MW01006745

EASY
HIRAGANA

First Steps to Reading and Writing
Basic Japanese

Fujihiko Kaneda

Calligraphy by Rika Samidori

Calligraphy Advisor
Takuya Dan

PASSPORT BOOKS
NTC/Contemporary Publishing Group

Also available
Easy Katakana

Cover design by Takashi Suzuki

This edition first published in 1989 by Passport Books,
a division of NTC Publishing Group,
4255 West Touhy Avenue, Lincolnwood (Chicago), Illinois 60646-1975 U.S.A.
Originally published by Yohan Publications, Inc. ©Yohan Publications, Inc.
Manufactured in the United States of America.

11 12 VRS/VRS 0 4

Contents

About the authors

Fujihiko Kaneda, a graduate of Osaka University of Foreign Studies, has been studying methods of teaching Japanese to foreign students and people who are interested in the Japanese language.

    Other books: Yohan English-Japanese, Japanese-English
                      Dictionary
                      Fuji-Tokaido

Takuya Dan, the headmaster of Japan Dynamic Calligraphy Society, created a new, original and highly stylized calligraphy in 1967, by revising the older Japanese forms.

    He has designed logos for many leading companies in Japan. His works have been shown at exhibitions in the main cities of the world.

    Other books: Dōsho (Dynamic Calligraphy)
                      Basic textbook for Dynamic Calligraphy

Rika Samidori, whose real name is Natsuyo Futatsugi, is a graduate of Kyōritsu Women's Junior College, and now works for Japan Air Lines. She has displayed her works in calligraphy exhibits in Paris, Montreal and Memphis, and in April '87 held her own show in Tokyo.

HOW TO WRITE JAPANESE

The writing system of Japanese consists of three types of symbols: Kanji, Hiragana and Katakana.

Kanji are Chinese characters and they were brought to Japan 2,000 years ago by Chinese Buddhist priests, and also by Japanese students and Japanese Buddhists, who had been studying in China. They were assimilated into the Japanese language and express ideas or concepts.

Hiragana and Katakana are phonetic symbols and represent pronunciation. The sounds they represent are similar to those of Spanish. They constitute a syllabary and represent the same sound or combination of sounds as are actually pronounced. They were created about 1,000 years ago by simplifying the Chinese characters or their parts, because the writing and reading of all words in Chinese characters was too difficult for the Japanese people.

Generally, we nowadays write Japanese by using Kanji and Hiragana. Katakana is used to express words of foreign origin—names of people, places, animals, plants, etc.

Hiragana is curvilinear in style and a little harder for foreigners to write than Katakana. But Hiragana is more important than Katakana in writing Japanese, as stated above, so it has to be learned first.

I would like to thank Ms. Rika Samidori, who wrote the sample calligraphy and also Mr. Takuya Dan, the headmaster of The Dynamic Calligraphy Society, who gave me invaluable suggestions for producing this book.

Fujihiko Kaneda

BASIC HIRAGANA

あ	か	さ	た	な
a	*ka*	*sa*	*ta*	*na*
い	き	し	ち	に
i	*ki*	*shi*	*chi*	*ni*
う	く	す	つ	ぬ
u	*ku*	*su*	*tsu*	*nu*
え	け	せ	て	ね
e	*ke*	*se*	*te*	*ne*
お	こ	そ	と	の
o	*ko*	*so*	*to*	*no*

は	ま	や	ら	わ
ha	*ma*	*ya*	*ra*	*wa*
ひ	み		り	
hi	*mi*		*ri*	
ふ	む	ゆ	る	
fu	*mu*	*yu*	*ru*	
へ	め		れ	
he	*me*		*re*	
ほ	も	よ	ろ	を
ho	*mo*	*yo*	*ro*	*o*
				ん
				n

The preceding table is called Gojū-on-zu (table of fifty sounds) in Japanese but *n* is considered soundless. Old Japanese employed more sounds/letters than the modern language; thus the blank squares in the chart.

The five letters (a, i, u, e, o) in the vertical line on the extreme left are vowels, ya, yu and yo are semi-vowels and the remaining syllables are consonants. Except for *n* and the five vowels, the syllables are romanized by a combination of a consonant and a vowel (ka, sa, etc.).

Each vertical line in this table is called *gyo* and is named by the top syllable of the line (a-gyo, ka-gyo, ga-gyo, etc.). Each horizontal line is called *dan* and are called a-dan, i-dan, u-dan, e-dan, and o-dan. At the bottom of the wa-gyo you will see another *o* sound but this *o* (を) is used only as the marker for the direct object particle.

Rōmaji (Romanization)

There are two systems in writing Japanese in Roman letters: *Hepburn (Hebon-shiki)* and *Official (Kunrei-shiki)*. The Hepburn system is used throughout this book as it is considered easier to use insofar as pronunciation is concerned.

▼ You will note that each page number is also written in Romanized Japanese and in Hiragana. Please practice writing these by copying them on a separate sheet of paper.

BASIC WAY OF WRITING

General stroke order in writing Hiragana
1. You write a horizontal line from left to right
2. You write a vertical line from top to bottom
Three ways to end a stroke
1. Tome (Stop)

   You stop the pen or pencil completely by pressing the paper slightly.

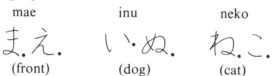

mae	inu	neko
(front)	(dog)	(cat)

2. Hane (Jump)

   You end the stroke with a small reflex tail in another direction.

kasa	take	hari
(umbrella)	(bamboo)	(needle)

3. Harai (Sweeping)

   You write this stroke by lifting the pen or pencil, gradually moving the hand to the end of the stroke.

ushi	tsume	asu
(cattle)	(finger nail)	(tomorrow)

The following explanation on the writing of Hiragana progresses gradually from the easier syllabary, which has fewer strokes, to the more difficult ones.

● Trace over the dotted examples, then fill in the exercise squares
  while referring to the numbers and arrows for instruction.

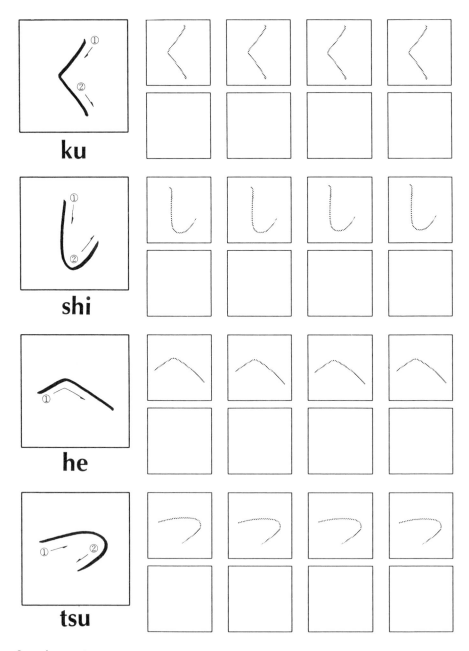

ku

shi

he

tsu

Note: Numbers indicate order of strokes to show beginners how to write easily, and do not always indicate the number of strokes.

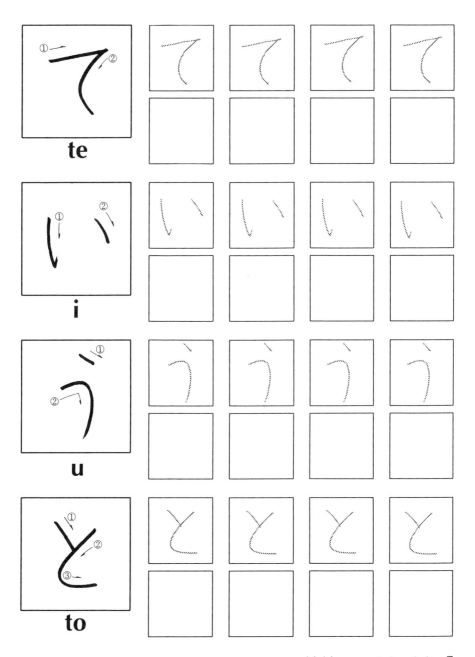

te

i

u

to

Exercises

● Trace over the dotted examples.

comb
ku · shi

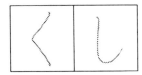

say
i · u

iron
te · tsu

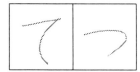

shoes
ku · tsu

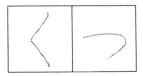

fence
he · i

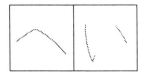

age
to · shi

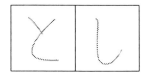

yarn
i · to

stone
i · shi

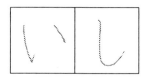

thrust
tsu · ku

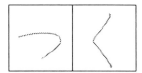

cattle
u · shi

when
i · tsu

stop
te · i · shi

door
to

at last
t · ō · t · ō

hit
u · tsu

soldier
he · i · shi

beautiful
u · tsu · ku · shi · i

hand
te

go
i · ku

four
shi

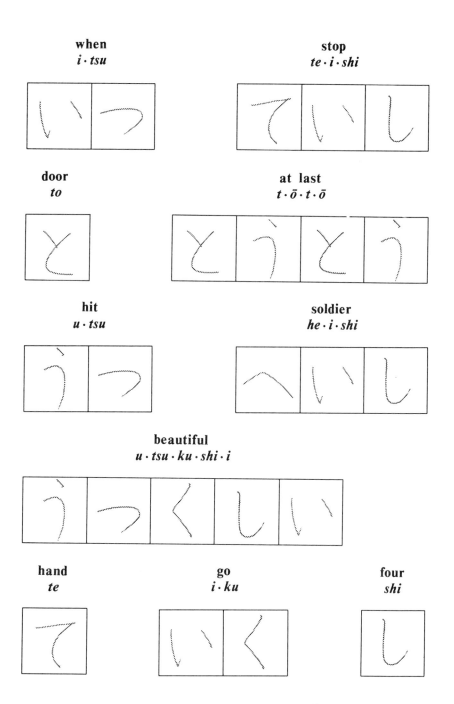

● Trace over the dotted examples, then fill in the exercise squares while referring to the numbers and arrows for instruction.

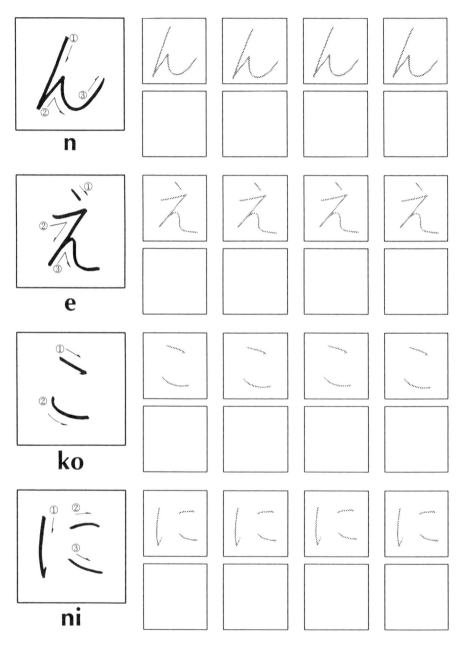

n

e

ko

ni

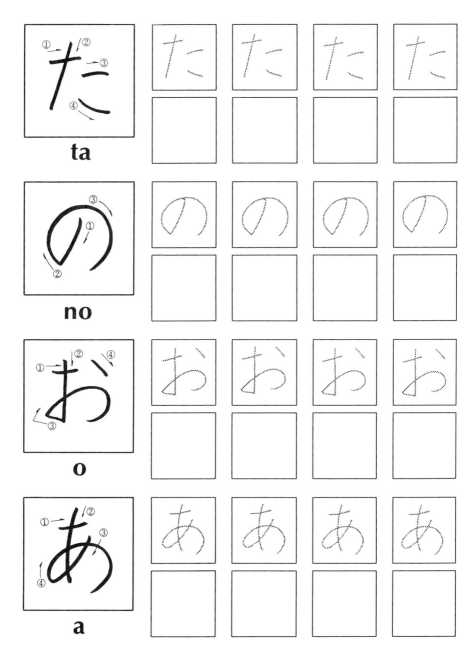

ta

no

o

a

Exercises

● Trace over the dotted examples.

west
ni · shi

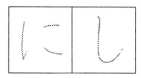

valley
ta · ni

voice
ko · e

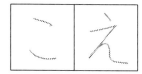

love
a · i

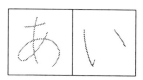

devil
o · ni

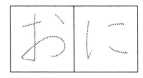

waist
ko · shi

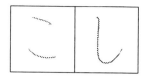

that
a · no

this
ko · no

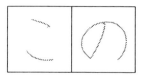

blue
a · o

dot
te · n

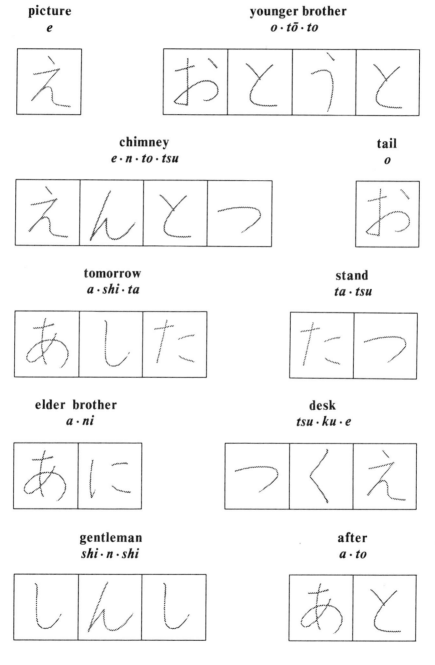

picture
e

え

younger brother
o · tō · to

お と う と

chimney
e · n · to · tsu

え ん と つ

tail
o

お

tomorrow
a · shi · ta

あ し た

stand
ta · tsu

た つ

elder brother
a · ni

あ に

desk
tsu · ku · e

つ く え

gentleman
shi · n · shi

し ん し

after
a · to

あ と

● Trace over the dotted examples, then fill in the exercise squares
while referring to the numbers and arrows for instruction.

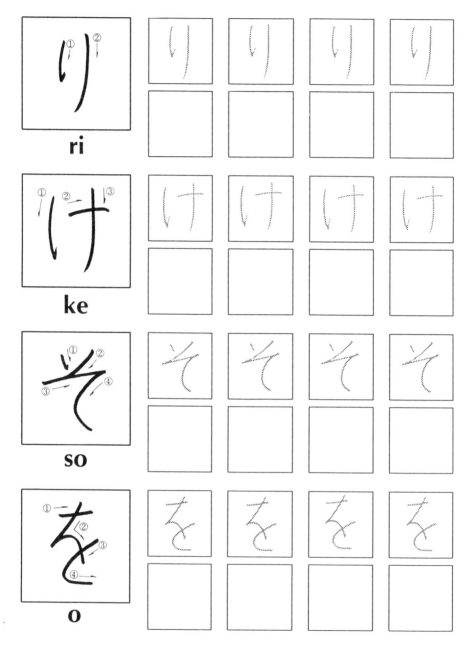

ri

ke

so

o

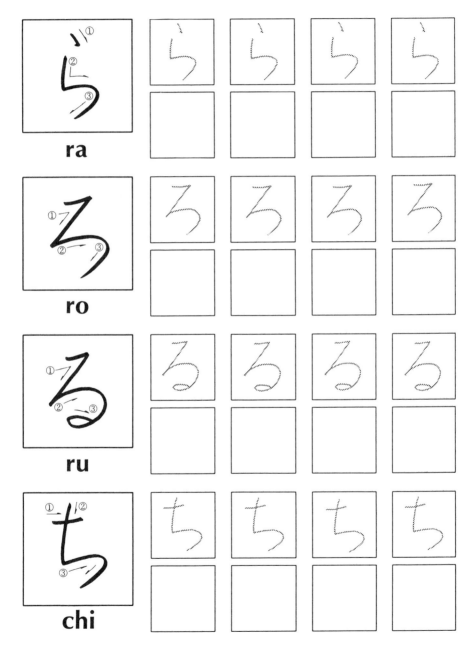

ra

ro

ru

chi

Exercises

● Trace over the dotted examples.

that
so · no

tub
o · ke

collar
e · ri

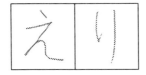

sky
so · ra

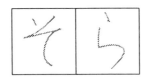

bamboo
ta · ke

tiger
to · ra

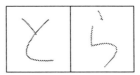

six
ro · ku

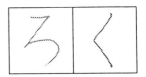

be
a · ru

boil
ni · ru

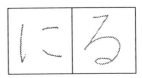

chestnut
ku · ri

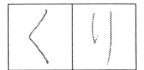

lion
ra · i · o · n

blood
chi

there
a · so · ko

home
u · chi

come
ku · ru

lesson
ke · i · ko

and
so · shi · te

here
ko · ko

later on
no · chi · ni

This *o* is used only as a particle.

● Trace over the dotted examples, then fill in the exercise squares
while referring to the numbers and arrows for instruction.

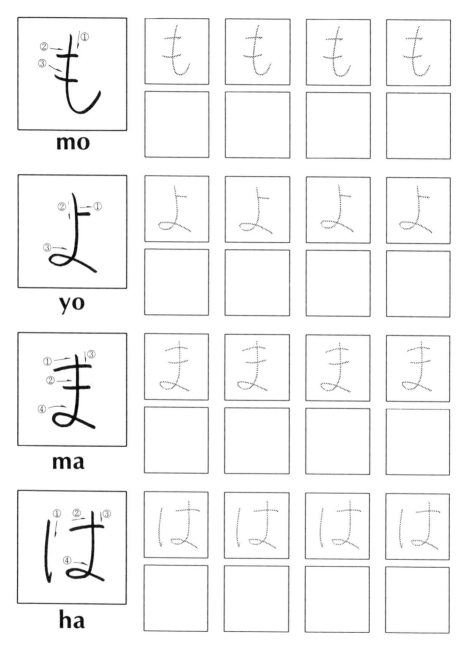

mo

yo

ma

ha

ho

na

mi

ka

Exercises

● Trace over the dotted examples.

gate
mo · n

good
yo · i

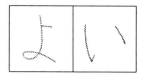

pine
ma · tsu

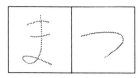

box
ha · ko

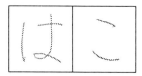

cheek
ho · ho

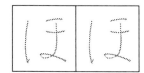

pear
na · shi

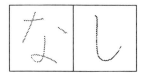

wave
na · mi

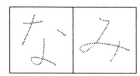

ear
mi · mi

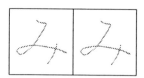

paper
ka · mi

face
ka · o

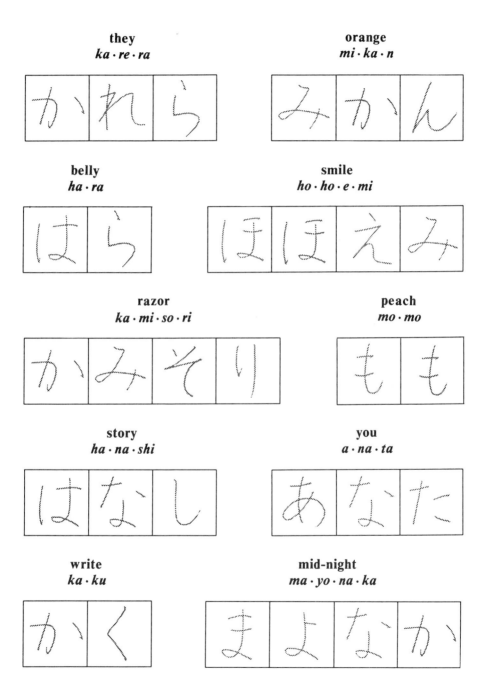

they
ka · re · ra

かれら

orange
mi · ka · n

みかん

belly
ha · ra

はら

smile
ho · ho · e · mi

ほほえみ

razor
ka · mi · so · ri

かみそり

peach
mo · mo

もも

story
ha · na · shi

はなし

you
a · na · ta

あなた

write
ka · ku

かく

mid-night
ma · yo · na · ka

まよなか

● Trace over the dotted examples, then fill in the exercise squares while referring to the numbers and arrows for instruction.

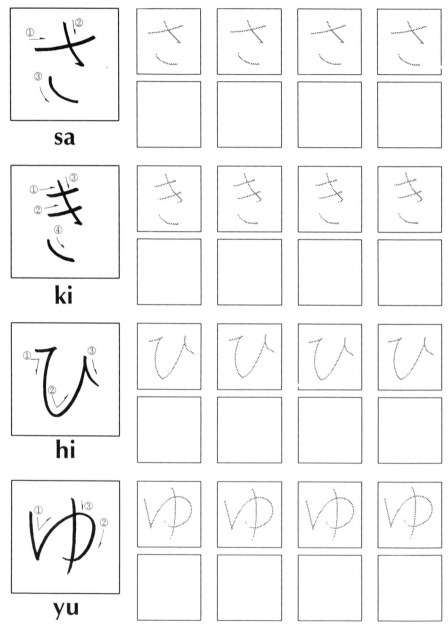

sa

ki

hi

yu

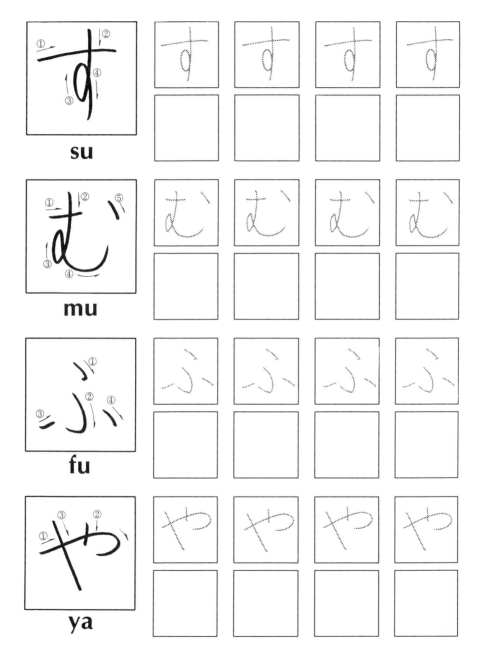

su

mu

fu

ya

Exercises

● Trace over the dotted examples.

chrysanthemum
ki · ku

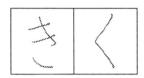

person
hi · to

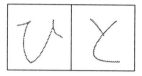

live
su · mu

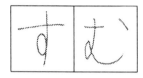

winter
fu · yu

autumn
a · ki

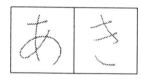

mountain
ya · ma

village
mu · ra

like
su · ki

liquor
sa · ke

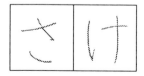

lily
yu · ri

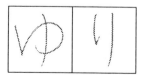

hot water
yu

noisy
ya·ka·ma·shi·i

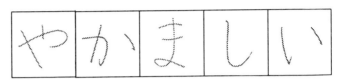

cherry
sa·ku·ra

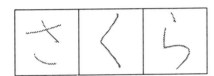

in the daytime
hi·ru·ma

pleasure
yu·ka·i

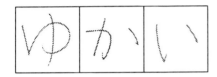

ancient
mu·ka·shi

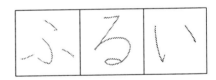

cheap
ya·su·i

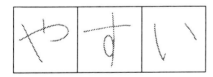

old
fu·ru·i

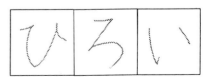

fox
ki·tsu·ne

wide
hi·ro·i

● Trace over the dotted examples, then fill in the exercise squares while referring to the numbers and arrows for instruction.

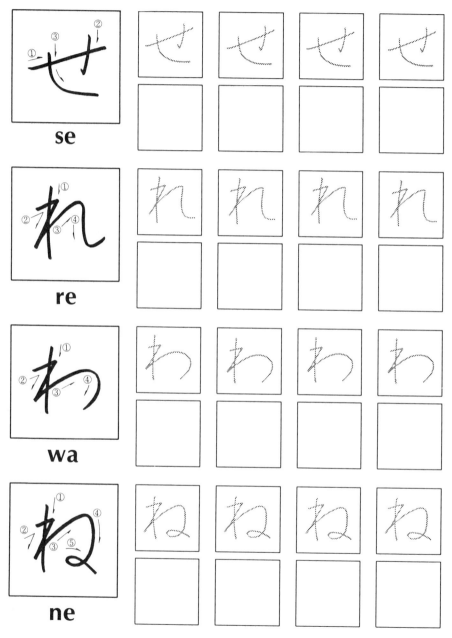

se

re

wa

ne

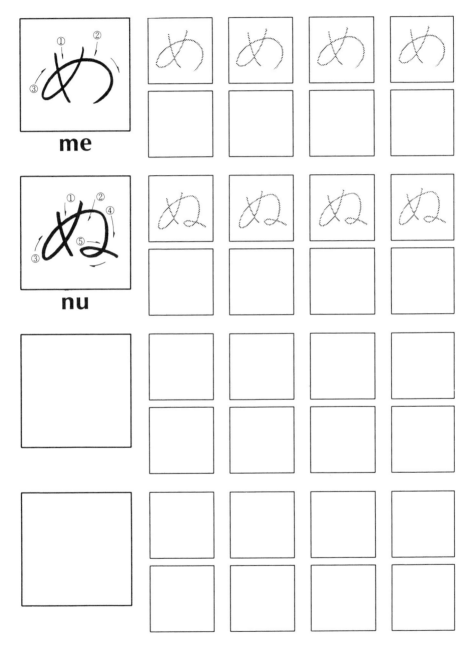

me

nu

Exercises

● Trace over the dotted examples.

dream
yu · me

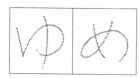

sew
nu · u

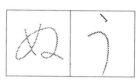

fine weather
ha · re

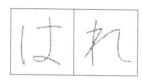

bride
yo · me

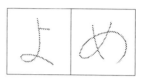

wrinkle
shi · wa

this
ko · re

shop
mi · se

silk
ki · nu

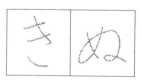

roof
ya · ne

cat
ne · ko

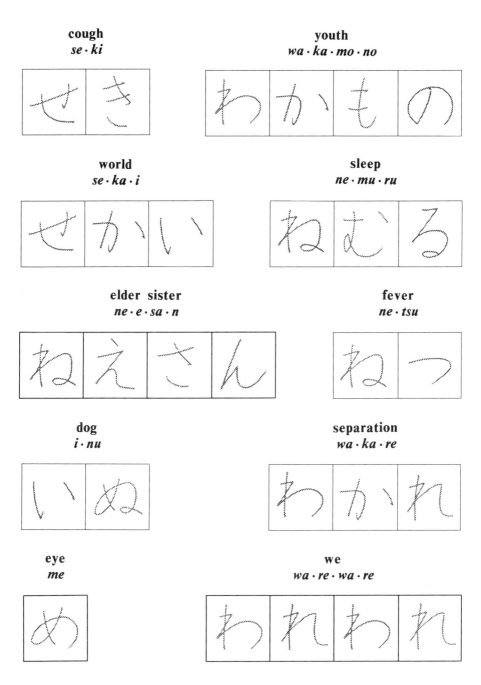

cough
se · ki

youth
wa · ka · mo · no

world
se · ka · i

sleep
ne · mu · ru

elder sister
ne · e · sa · n

fever
ne · tsu

dog
i · nu

separation
wa · ka · re

eye
me

we
wa · re · wa · re

Voiced and Semi-Voiced Syllables
(Dakuon and Han-Dakuon)

Ka-gyo	か ka	き ki	く ku	け ke	こ ko
Ga-gyo	が ga	ぎ gi	ぐ gu	げ ge	ご go

Examples:

がくせい *gakusei* (student)   ぎんこう *ginkō* (bank)

ぬぐ *nugu* (take off)   げんき *genki* (vigor)

ごご *gogo* (afternoon)

Sa-gyo	さ sa	し shi	す su	せ se	そ so
Za-gyo	ざ za	じ ji	ず zu	ぜ ze	ぞ zo

Examples:

ひざ *hiza* (knee)   じかん *jikan* (time)

かず *kazu* (number)   かぜ *kaze* (wind)

ぞくご *zokugo* (slang)

Ta-gyo	た ta	ち chi	つ tsu	て te	と to
Da-gyo	だ da	ぢ ji	づ zu	で de	ど do

Examples:

だいこん *daikon* (radish)   はなぢ *hanaji* (nosebleed)

つづく *tsuzuku* (continue)   できる *dekiru* (can)

どこ *doko* (where)

Ha-gyo	は ha	ひ hi	ふ fu	へ he	ほ ho
Ba-gyo	ば ba	び bi	ぶ bu	べ be	ぼ bo
Pa-gyo	ぱ pa	ぴ pi	ぷ pu	ぺ pe	ぽ po

Examples:

けいば *keiba* (horse racing)   かび *kabi* (mold)

ぶた *buta* (pig)   なべ *nabe* (pan)

ぼうし *bōshi* (hat)   とっぱつ *toppatsu* (outbreak)

がっぴ *gappi* (date)   とっぷう *toppū* (gust)

がっぺい *gappei*   いっぽ *ippo* (a pace)
　　　　(amalgamation)

The above basic syllables of Ka-gyo, Sa-gyo, Ta-gyo and Ha-gyo are changed to voiced syllables by adding two short strokes (゛) on the upper right part of each syllable in Hiragana.

For example:

か ＋ ゛ ＝ が　　さ ＋ ゛ ＝ ざ
ka　　　　　　ga　　sa　　　　　　za

The semi-voiced syllables of Ha-gyo (ha, hi, fu, he and ho) are pa, pi, pu, pe and po. They are written in Hiragana by putting a small circle (°) on the upper right part of each syllable.

は ＋ ° ＝ ぱ　ほ ＋ ° ＝ ぽ
ha　　　　　pa　ho　　　　　po

The voiced syllables for し (shi) and ち (chi) are じ (ji) and ぢ (ji), which are pronounced the same; as is the case with the voiced syllables for す (su) and つ (tsu). As a general rule, in modern Japanese じ (ji) is used commonly for both じ (ji) and ぢ (ji) and ず (zu) is used for both ず (zu) and づ (zu).

However, ぢ (ji) and づ (zu) are still used in a few cases as in the following examples:

1. In a compound word in which the first syllable of the second word is ち (chi), it changes to a voiced sound as a result of euphonic change, ぢ (ji), not じ (ji):

はな ＋ ち ＝ はなぢ
hana　*chi*　*hanaji*
nose　blood　nosebleed

In the same way, if the first syllable of the second word is つ (tsu), it changes to a voiced sound づ (zu), not ず (zu) due to euphonic change.

み（っ）か ＋ つき ＝ みかづき
mi(k)ka　*tsuki*　*mikazuki*
third day　moon　crescent (moon)

2. In case ち (chi) and つ (tsu) change to voiced sounds in a word due to repetition of the syllable, the first ち (chi) or つ (tsu) is not changed, but the following ち (chi) or つ (tsu) becomes voiced: ぢ (ji) or づ (zu) respectively.

ちぢむ
chijimu (shrink)

つづく
tsuzuku (continue)

Please take note of the following rules:

In a compound word, in cases where the first letter of the second word is *k, s, t,* or *h* they are sometimes voiced as *g, z, d,* or *b* respectively by compound and euphonic change.

Ka-gyo ⟶ Ga-gyo   か-ぎょう → が-ぎょう

うみ ＋ かめ ＝ うみがめ

umi	*kame*	*umigame*
sea	turtle	(sea) turtle

みず ＋ き ＝ みずぎ

mizu	*ki*	*mizugi*
water	suit	swimming suit

なが(い) ＋ くつ ＝ ながぐつ

naga(i)	*kutsu*	*nagagutsu*
long	shoes	boots

きょうだい＋けんか＝きょうだい
げんか

kyōdai
siblings

kenka
quarrel

kyōdai-genka
sibling quarrels

やま ＋ こや ＝ やまごや

yama
mountain

koya
hut

yamagoya
mountain hut

<u>Sa-gyo</u> → <u>Za-gyo</u>   <u>さ-ぎょう</u> → <u>ざ-ぎょう</u>

こ ＋ さら ＝ こざら

ko
small

sara
plate

kozara
small plate

たから ＋ しま ＝ たからじま

takara
treasure

shima
island

takarajima
treasure island

にぎり ＋ すし ＝ にぎりずし

nigiri
hand-rolled

sushi
sushi

nigirizushi
hand-rolled **sushi**

ひゃくにち＋せき＝ひゃくにちぜき

hyakunichi
one hundred days

seki
cough

hyakunichizeki
whooping cough

ゆう（がた）＋ そら ＝ ゆうぞら

yū (gata)
evening

sora
sky

yūzora
evening sky

Ta-gy<u>o</u> → Da-gy<u>o</u>　　　た-ぎょう → だ-ぎょう

おお（きい）＋ たる ＝ おおだる

ō (kii)
big

taru
cask

ōdaru
butt

はな ＋ ち ＝ はなぢ

hana
nose

chi
blood

hanaji
nosebleed

ふろしき＋つつみ＝ふろしきづつみ

furoshiki
wrapping cloth

tsutsumi
package

furoshikizutsumi
cloth wrapped parcel

みず ＋ てっぽう ＝ みずでっぽう

mizu
water

teppō
gun

mizudeppō
squirt-gun

うで ＋ とけい ＝ うでどけい

ude
wrist

tokei
watch

udedokei
wrist watch

Ha-gyo → Ba-gyo   は-ぎょう → ば-ぎょう

ほん ＋ はこ ＝ ほんばこ

hon
book

hako
case

honbako
bookcase

ね ＋ ひき ＝ ねびき

ne
price

hiki
cut down

nebiki
discount

かみ ＋ ふくろ ＝ かみぶくろ

kami
paper

fukuro
bag

kamibukuro
paper bag

いた ＋ へい ＝ いたべい

ita
board

hei
fence

itabei
board fence

ひと ＋ ひと ＝ ひとびと

hito
person

hito
person

hitobito
people

● Trace over the dotted lines.

Exercises

egg
ta·ma·go

school
ga·kko

brick
re·n·ga

look for
sa·ga·su

dust
go·mi

student
ga·ku·se·i

make a noise
sa·wa·gu

move
u·go·ku

June
ro·ku-ga·tsu

take off
nu·gu

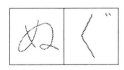

view
na · ga · me

な が め

saw
no · ka · gi · ri

の こ ぎ り

army
gu · n · ta · i

ぐ ん た い

run away
ni · ge · ru

に げ る

grasp
ni · gi · ru

に ぎ る

wages
chi · n · gi · n

ち ん ぎ ん

gold
ō · go · n

お う ご ん

scorch
ko · ge · ru

こ げ る

English
e · i · go

え い ご

loud voice
ō · go · e

お お ご え

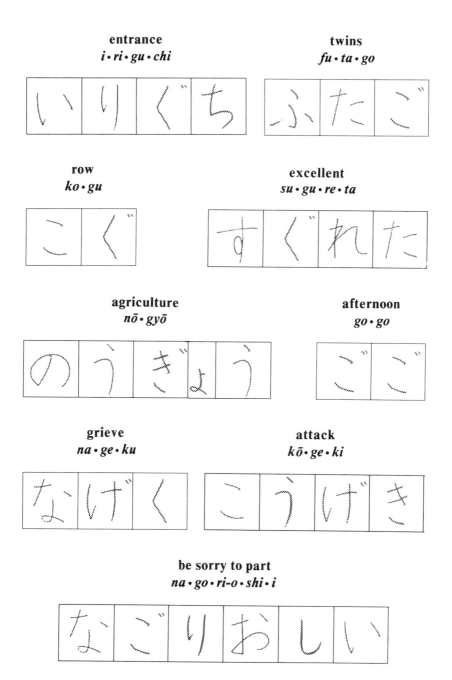

entrance
i・ri・gu・chi

twins
fu・ta・go

row
ko・gu

excellent
su・gu・re・ta

agriculture
nō・gyō

afternoon
go・go

grieve
na・ge・ku

attack
kō・ge・ki

be sorry to part
na・go・ri-o・shi・i

nail (metal)
ku・gi

くぎ

comfort
na・gu・sa・me・ru

なぐさめる

direction
ho・u・ga・ku

ほうがく

spirits (health)
ge・n・ki

げんき

postcard
ha・ga・ki

はがき

at present
ge・n・za・i

げんざい

silver
gi・n

ぎん

(internal) medicine
no・mi・gu・su・ri

のみぐすり

wheat
mu・gi

むぎ

laughing voice
wa・ra・i・go・e

わらいごえ

polish
mi・ga・ku

みがく

music
o・n・ga・ku

おんがく

smell
ka・gu

かぐ

thank you
a・ri・ga・tō

ありがとう

theater
ge・ki・jō

げきじょう

next
tsu・gi

つぎ

work
sa・gyō

さぎょう

interrupt
sa・e・gi・ru

さえぎる

cash
ge・n・ki・n

げんきん

bank check
ko・gi・tte

こぎって

Za-gyō ざ-ぎょう

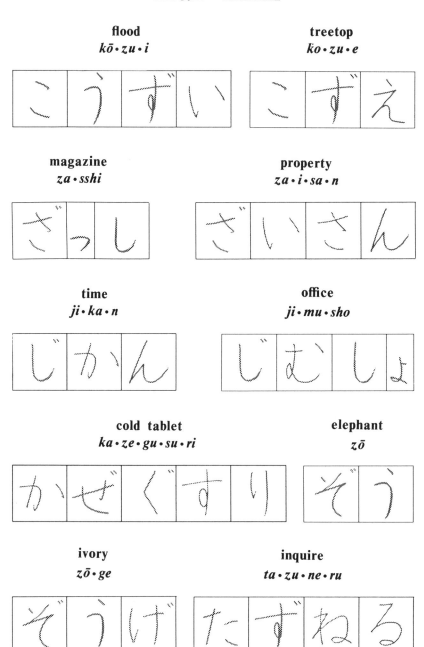

flood
kō・zu・i

こうずい

treetop
ko・zu・e

こずえ

magazine
za・sshi

ざっし

property
za・i・sa・n

ざいさん

time
ji・ka・n

じかん

office
ji・mu・sho

じむしょ

cold tablet
ka・ze・gu・su・ri

かぜぐすり

elephant
zō

ぞう

ivory
zō・ge

ぞうげ

inquire
ta・zu・ne・ru

たずねる

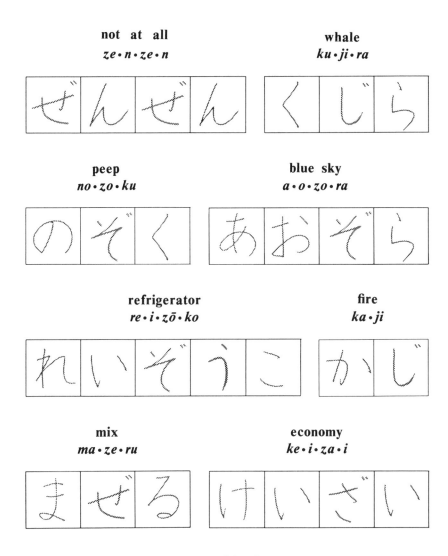

not at all
ze・n・ze・n

ぜ ん ぜ ん

whale
ku・ji・ra

く じ ら

peep
no・zo・ku

の ぞ く

blue sky
a・o・zo・ra

あ お そ ら

refrigerator
re・i・zō・ko

れ い ぞ う こ

fire
ka・ji

か じ

mix
ma・ze・ru

ま ぜ る

economy
ke・i・za・i

け い ざ い

old friend
mu・ka・shi-na・ji・mi

む か し な じ み

difficult
mu・zu・ka・shi・i

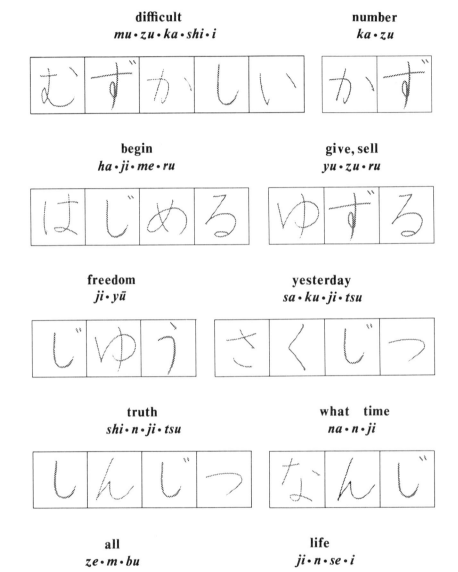

number
ka・zu

begin
ha・ji・me・ru

give, sell
yu・zu・ru

freedom
ji・yū

yesterday
sa・ku・ji・tsu

truth
shi・n・ji・tsu

what　time
na・n・ji

all
ze・m・bu

life
ji・n・se・i

be ashamed
ha・zu・ka・shi・i

uncle
o・ji

cool
su・zu・shi・i

volcano
ka・za・n

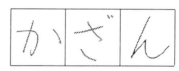

ago
i・ze・n

at most
se・i・ze・i

safety
a・n・ze・n

custom house
ze・i・ka・n

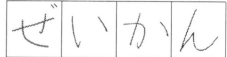

remarkable
i・chi・ji・ru・shi・i

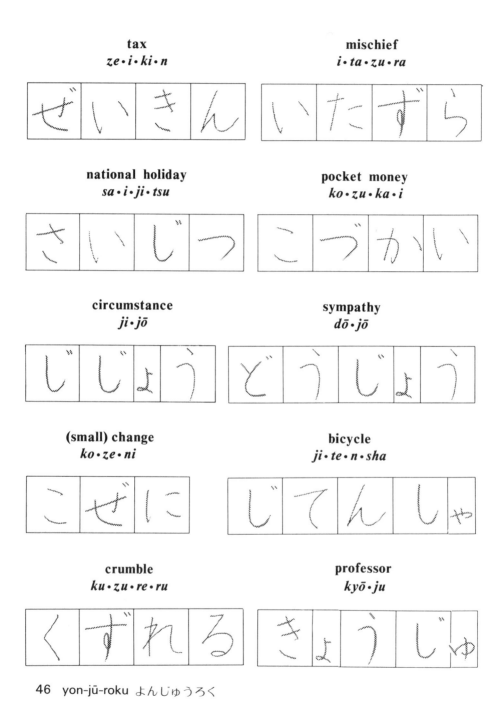

tax
ze・i・ki・n

mischief
i・ta・zu・ra

national holiday
sa・i・ji・tsu

pocket money
ko・zu・ka・i

circumstance
ji・jō

sympathy
dō・jō

(small) change
ko・ze・ni

bicycle
ji・te・n・sha

crumble
ku・zu・re・ru

professor
kyō・ju

Da-gyō だ-ぎょう

friend
to・mo・da・chi

ともだち

this[next] time
ko・n・do

こんど

please
dō・zo

どうぞ

menu
ko・n・da・te

こんだて

right
ta・da・shi・i

ただしい

how
dō

どう

barefoot
ha・da・shi

はだし

parcel
ko・zu・tsu・mi

こづつみ

underwear
ha・da・gi

はだぎ

new moon
mi・ka・zu・ki

みかづき

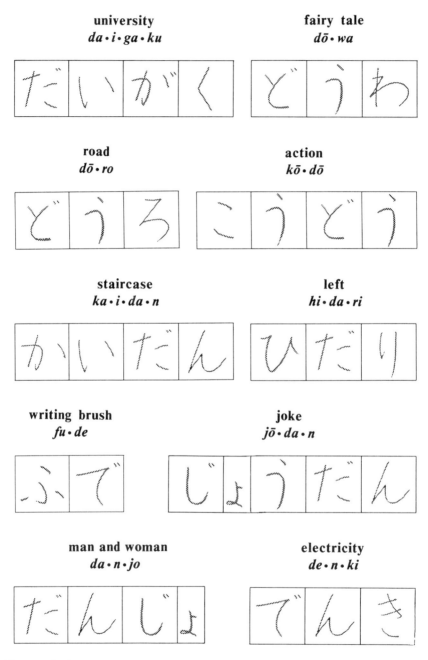

university
da・i・ga・ku

だ い が く

fairy tale
dō・wa

ど う わ

road
dō・ro

ど う ろ

action
kō・dō

こ う ど う

staircase
ka・i・da・n

か い だ ん

left
hi・da・ri

ひ だ り

writing brush
fu・de

ふ で

joke
jō・da・n

じょ う だ ん

man and woman
da・n・jo

だ ん じょ

electricity
de・n・ki

で ん き

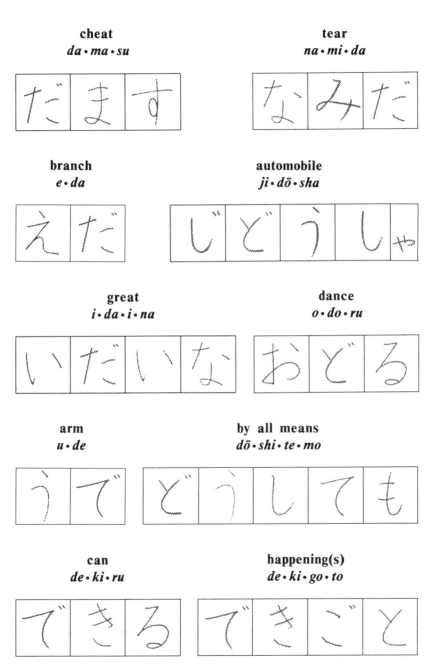

cheat
da·ma·su

だます

tear
na·mi·da

なみだ

branch
e·da

えだ

automobile
ji·dō·sha

じどうしゃ

great
i·da·i·na

いだいな

dance
o·do·ru

おどる

arm
u·de

うで

by all means
dō·shi·te·mo

どうしても

can
de·ki·ru

できる

happening(s)
de·ki·go·to

できごと

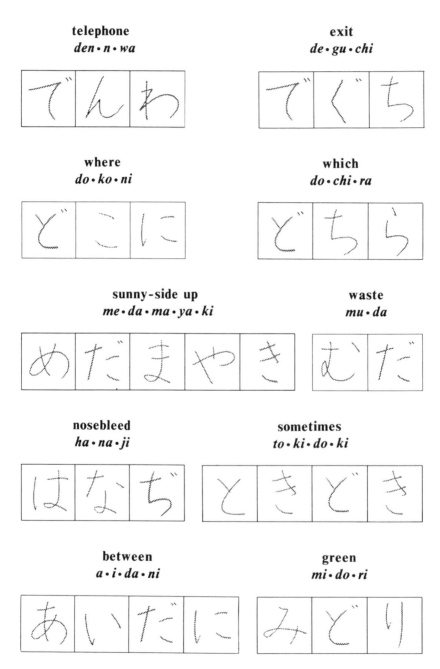

telephone
den・n・wa

でんわ

exit
de・gu・chi

でぐち

where
do・ko・ni

どこに

which
do・chi・ra

どちら

sunny-side up
me・da・ma・ya・ki

めだまやき

waste
mu・da

むだ

nosebleed
ha・na・ji

はなぢ

sometimes
to・ki・do・ki

ときどき

between
a・i・da・ni

あいだに

green
mi・do・ri

みどり

Ba-gyō ば-ぎょう

hat
bō・shi

ぼうし

this evening
ko・m・ba・n

こんばん

get tired
ku・ta・bi・re・ru

くたびれる

wall
ka・be

かべ

drama
shi・ba・i

しばい

lip
ku・chi・bi・ru

くちびる

stockholder
ka・bu・nu・shi

かぶぬし

press, wring
shi・bo・ru

しぼる

climb
no・bo・ru

のぼる

newspaper
shi・m・bu・n

しんぶん

bag
ka・ba・n

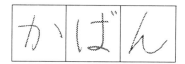

thumb
o・ya・yu・bi

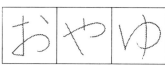

again
fu・ta・ta・bi

inconvenience
fu・be・n

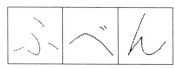

fireworks
ha・na・bi

bouquet
ha・na・ta・ba

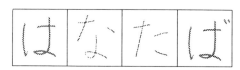

half
ha・m・bu・n

apologize
wa・bi・ru

post office
yū・bi・n・kyo・ku

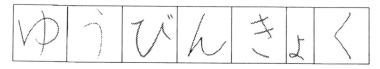

neck
ku・bi

くび

lawyer
be・n・go・shi

べんごし

reward
hō・bi

ぼうび

horse race
ke・i・ba

けいば

cry
sa・ke・bu

さけぶ

decayed tooth
mu・shi・ba

むしば

lonesome
sa・bi・shi・i

さびしい

pot
na・be

なべ

after a long time
hi・sa・shi・bu・ri・ni

ひさしぶりに

perhaps
ta・bu・n

cover
ka・bu・se・ru

villa
be・ssō

eat
ta・be・ru

desert
sa・ba・ku

slip
su・be・ru

yawn
a・ku・bi

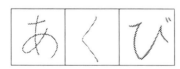

part
bu・bu・n

inside
na・i・bu

bind
shi・ba・ru

oneself
ji • bu • n

often
ta • bi • ta • bi

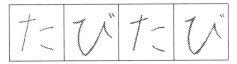

living thing
se • i • bu • tsu

select
e • ra • bu

all
su • be • te

unskillful
bu • ki • yō

kiosk
ba • i • ten

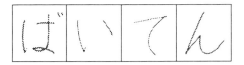

I am
Bo • ku ha

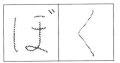

bottle
bi • n

writing pad
bi • n • se • n

Pa-gyō   ぱ-ぎょう

Japanese deep-fried food
te・m・pu・ra

てんぷら

progress
shi・m・po

しんぽ

stroll
sa・m・po

さんぽ

worry
shi・m・pa・i

しんぱい

new article
shi・m・pi・n

しんぴん

(something) incomplete
ha・m・pa

はんぱ

pull
hi・ppa・ru

ひっぱる

dandelion
ta・m・po・po

たんぽぽ

mischievous
wa・m・pa・ku・na

わんぱくな

ticket
ki・ppu

きっぷ

grammar
bu・m・pō

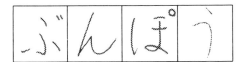

mystery
shi・m・pi

father (priest)
shi・m・pu

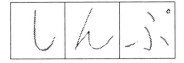

repulsion
ha・m・pa・tsu

publication
shu・ppa・n

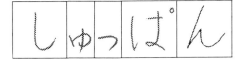

installment plan
ge・ppu

frequently
hi・m・pa・n・ni

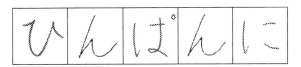

announce
ha・ppyō・su・ru

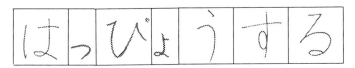

satisfied (with full stomach)
ma · m · pu · ku

Japan
Ni · ppo · n

gun
te · ppō

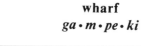

wharf
ga · m · pe · ki

measurement
su · m · pō

expenses
shu · ppi

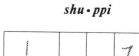

electric wave
de · m · pa

telegram
de · m · pō

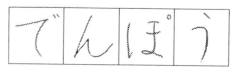

divide
bu · m · pa · i-su · ru

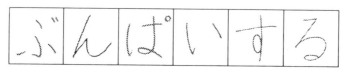

cube
ri・ppō・ta・i

packing
ko・m・pō

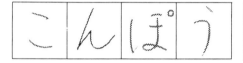

departure
shu・ppa・tsu

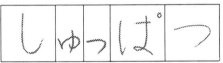

lively
ka・ppa・tsu・na

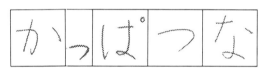

constitution
ke・m・pō

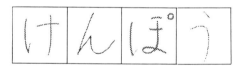

splendid
ri・ppa・na

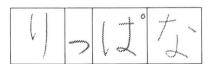

fundamental
ko・m・po・n・te・ki

general
i • ppa • n • no

medical compress
shi • ppu

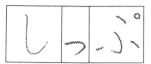

toast (cheers!)
ka • m • pa • i

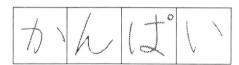

union
ga • ppe • i

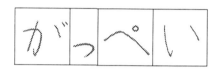

umpire
shi • m • pa • n

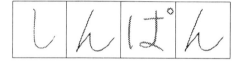

failure
shi • ppa • i

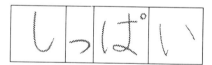

perfect
ka • m • pe • ki • na

tail
shi • ppo

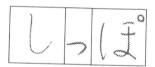

be refreshed
sa • ppa • ri • su • ru

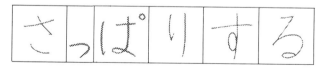

Long Vowels (Chōon)

Romanized long vowels are usually shown with a macron over the vowel as in *ō* and *ū* in particular. *Ō* and *ū* are the most common long vowels and *ō* is sometimes also written as *oo*.

The long *a* can be written as *ā* or aa.

The long *i* is written as *ii*. With the exception of a few words like *oneesan* おねえさん (elder sister), there is no occurence of a long *e* in Japanese. *E* and *i*, however, are frequently combined as a dipthong, as in *eigo* えいご (English), *Beikoku* べいこく (USA) and so on. For all practical purposes, it is best to think of only *o* and *u* as the most frequently used long vowels in Japanese.

Many loan words from English and other foreign languages include a long vowel in them and the words are usually written in Katakana. Since this book is for learning written Hiragana, they are shown in both Hiragana and Katakana.

1. Syllables of *a-dan* （あ・だん）

The long sound of the syllables of *a-dan* （あ・だん） is shown by adding あ(*a*) to the basic sound in Hiragana.

Basic sounds	あ a	か ka	さ sa	た ta	な na	は ha	ま ma	や ya	ら ra	わ wa
Long sounds	ああ ā aa	かあ kā kaa	さあ sā saa	たあ tā taa	なあ nā naa	はあ hā haa	まあ mā maa	やあ yā yaa	らあ rā raa	わあ wā waa

Examples:

ああ　*Ā*(Ah!)　　　　　　　おかあさん　*okāsan* (mother)
　　Aa　　　　　　　　　　　　*okaasan*

さあ　*sā*(come on, now)　　たあみなる, ターミナル　*tāminaru* (terminal)
　　saa　　　　　　　　　　　　　*taaminaru*

なあす,　ナース　*nāsu* (nurse)　　はあと, ハート　*hāto* (heart)
　　　　　　naasu　　　　　　　　　　　*haato*

まあち, マーチ　*māchi* (march)　　やあ　*Yā* (Hello)
　　　　maachi　　　　　　　　　*Yaa*

らあめん,ラーメン　*rāmen* (Chinese noodles)　わあ　*Wā* (Hurrah!)
　　　　raamen　　　　　　　　　　　　　　*Waa*

Basic sounds		が ga	ざ za	だ da	ば ba	ぱ pa
Long sounds		があ *gā* gaa	ざあ *zā* zaa	だあ *dā* daa	ばあ *bā* baa	ぱあ *pā* paa

Examples:

がある・ふれんど, ガール・フレンド　*gāru-furendo* (girl friend)
　　　　　　　　　　gaaru-furendo

があがあ　*gāgā* (quack)　　　　ざあざあ　*zāzā* (pour down)
　　　gaagaa　　　　　　　　　　*zaazaa*

だあす, ダース　*dāsu* (dozen)　　おばあさん　*obāsan* (grandmother)
　　　　daasu　　　　　　　　　　*obaasan*

ぱあせんと, パーセント　*pāsento* (per cent)
　　　　　paasento

2. Syllables of *i-dan* （い・だん）

The long sound of the syllables of *i-dan* （い・だん） is shown by adding い *(i)* to the basic sound in Hiragana.

Basic sounds	い i	き ki	し shi	ち chi	に ni	ひ hi	み mi	り ri
Long sounds	いい ii	きい kii	しい shii	ちい chii	にい nii	ひい hii	みい mii	りい rii

Examples:

いいわけ *iiwake* (excuse)

きいきい *kiikii* (squeaky)

しいつ, シーツ *shiitsu* (sheet)

ちいさい *chiisai* (small)

おにいさん *oniisan* (elder brother)

ひいき *hiiki* (favor)

みいてぃんぐ, ミーティング *miitingu* (meeting)

りいだあ, リーダー *Riidā* (leader)

Basic sounds		ぎ gi	じ ji	ぢ ji		び bi	ぴ pi
Long sounds		ぎい gii	じい jii	ぢい jii		びい bii	ぴい pii

Examples:

ぎいぎい *giigii* (creak)

おじいさん *ojiisan* (grandfather)

びいる, ビール *biiru* (beer)

ぴいぴい *piipii* (whistle)

3. Syllables of *u-dan* (う・だん)

The long sound of the syllables of *u-dan* (う・だん) is shown by adding う *(u)* to the basic sound in Hiragana.

Basic sounds	う u	く ku	す su	つ tsu	ぬ nu	ふ fu	む mu	ゆ yu	る ru
Long sounds	うう ū	くう kū	すう sū	つう tsū	ぬう nū	ふう fū	むう mū	ゆう yū	るう rū

Examples:

ううる, ウール *ūru* (wool)　　　　くうき *kūki* (air)

すうじ *sūji* (number)　　　　　　つうろ *tsūro* (passage)

ぬうど, ヌード *nūdo* (nude)　　　ふうふ *fūfu* (married couple)

むうど, ムード *mūdo* (mood)　　ゆうかんな *yūkan'na* (brave)

るうる, ルール *rūru* (rule)

Basic sounds		ぐ gu	ず zu	づ zu	ぶ bu	ぷ pu
Long sounds		ぐう gū	ずう zū	づう zū	ぶう bū	ぷう pū

Examples:

ぐうぐう *gūgū* (be fast asleep)　ずうずうしい *zūzūshii* (impudent)

ぶうむ, ブーム *būmu* (boom)　ぷうる, プール *pūru* (pool)

4. Syllables of *o-dan* (お・だん)

The long sound of the syllables of *o-dan* (お・だん) is shown by adding う (*u*) to the basic sound in Hiragana.

Basic sounds	お o	こ ko	そ so	と to	の no	ほ no	も mo	よ yo	ろ ro
Long sounds	おう ō oo	こう kō koo	そう sō soo	とう tō too	のう nō noo	ほう hō hoo	もう mō moo	よう yō yoo	ろう rō roo

Examples:

おうじ *ōji* (prince) こうえん *kōen* (park)

そうじ *sōji* (cleaning) とうとう *tōtō* (at last)

のうか *nōka* (farmer) ほうれんそう *hōrensō* (spinach)

もうしこむ *mōshikomu* (apply for) ようい *yōi* (preparation)

ろうじん *rōjin* (old man)

Basic sounds		ご go	ぞ zo	ど do		ぼ bo	ぽ po
Long sounds		ごう gō goo	ぞう zō zoo	どう dō doo		ぼう bō boo	ぽう pō poo

Examples:

ごうけい *gōkei* (total) ぞう *zō* (elephant)

どうして *dōshite* (why, how) ぼうし *bōshi* (hat)

でんぽう *dempō* (telegram)

As an exception to the rule for the long vowel of the syllable of
o-dan (お・だん) in Hiragana, instead of う (*u*) お (*o*) is used in
some words.

おおきい *ō・ki・i* (big)   おおい *ō・i* (many)
    o・o・ki・i   *o・o・i*

こおり *kō・ri* (ice)   こおる *kō・ru* (freeze)
    ko・o・ri   *ko・o・ru*

とおい *tō・i* (far, distant)   とおく *tō・ku* (far away)
    to・o・i   *to・o・ku*

とおり *tō・ri* (street)   とおる *tō・ru* (pass)
    to・o・ri   *to・o・ru*

とお *tō* (ten)   とおか *tō・ka* (10th day of the month)
    to・o   *to・o・ka*

おおかみ *ō・ka・mi* (wolf) こおろぎ *kō・ro・gi* (grasshopper)
    o・o・ka・mi   *ko・o・ro・gi*

● Trace over the dotted lines.

Exercises

broadcast
hō・sō・su・ru

father
o・tō・sa・n

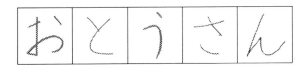

mother
o・kā・sa・n

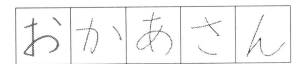

grandmother
o・bā・sa・n

ten
tō

trade
bō・e・ki

air
kū・ki

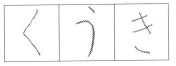

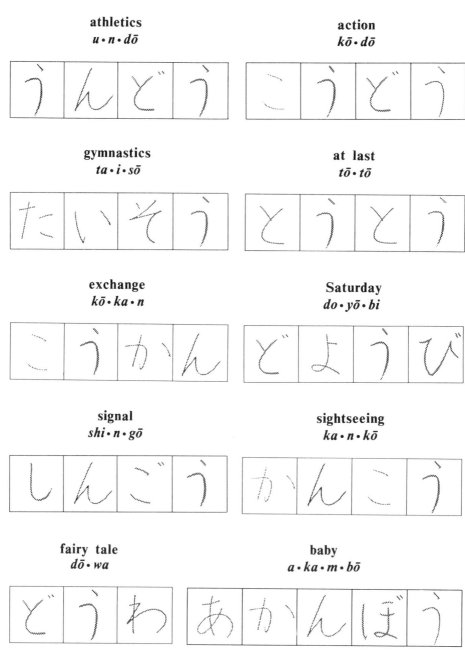

athletics
u · n · dō

うんどう

action
kō · dō

こうどう

gymnastics
ta · i · sō

たいそう

at last
tō · tō

とうとう

exchange
kō · ka · n

こうかん

Saturday
do · yō · bi

どようび

signal
shi · n · gō

しんごう

sightseeing
ka · n · kō

かんこう

fairy tale
dō · wa

どうわ

baby
a · ka · m · bō

あかんぼう

December
jū · ni-ga · tsu

nursery rhyme
dō · yō

airplane
hi · kō · ki

perfume
kō · su · i

park
kō · e · n

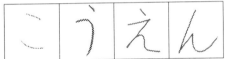

like this
ko · no · yō · ni

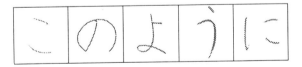

traffic accident
kō · tsū · ji · ko

the Crown Prince
kō・ta・i・shi

effect
kō・ka

by chance
gū・ze・n・ni

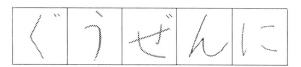

method
hō・hō

fifty
go・jū

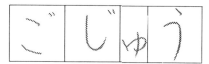

direction
hō・ga・ku

adventure
bō・ke・n

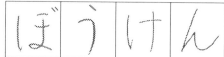

high school
kō・tō・ga・kkō

friendship
yū·jo

ゆ　う　じょ　う

ice
kō·ri

こ　お　り

brave
yū·ka·n·na

ゆ　う　か　ん　な

public
ō·ya·ke·no

お　お　や　け　の

evening
yū·ga·ta

ゆ　う　が　た

freeze
kō·ru

こ　お　る

many
ō·i

お　お　い

big
ō·ki·i

お　お　き　い

wolf
ō・ka・mi

おおかみ

far, distant
tō・i

とおい

pass
tō・ru

とおる

candle
rō・so・ku

ろうそく

wind bell
fū・ri・n

ふうりん

(married) couple
fū・fu

ふうふ

sweeping
sō・ji

そうじ

law
hō・ri・tsu

ほうりつ

post office
yū・bi・n・kyo・ku

ゆうびんきょく

bank
gi · n · kō

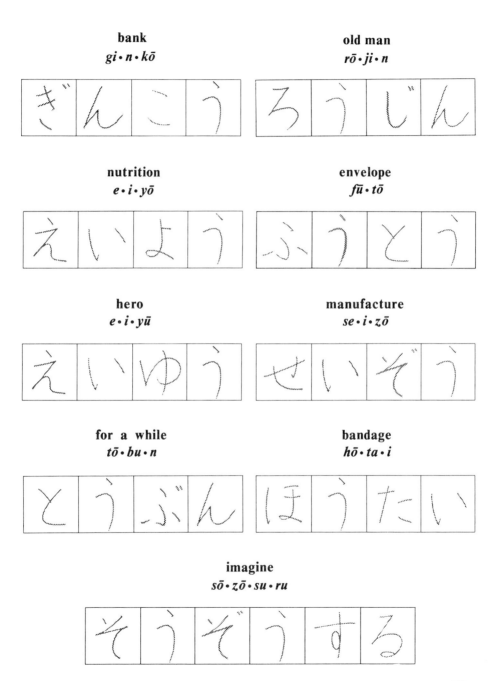

ぎ ん こ う

old man
rō · ji · n

ろ う じ ん

nutrition
e · i · yō

え い よ う

envelope
fū · tō

ふ う と う

hero
e · i · yū

え い ゆ う

manufacture
se · i · zō

せ い ぞ う

for a while
tō · bu · n

と う ぶ ん

bandage
hō · ta · i

ほ う た い

imagine
sō · zō · su · ru

そ う ぞ う す る

Double Consonants (Sokuon)

Double consonants occur in a word in which the pronunciation of a vowel stops suddenly and the following syllable begins with h, k, s, t, or p. A very simple and systematic rule exists for writing double consonants in Hiragana and Katakana except n and m. Double consonants are preceded by small つ (tsu) and these consonants are given strong (double) force in pronunciation.

Ka-gyo	っか -kka	っき -kki	っく -kku	っけ -kke	っこ -kko

Examples:

さっか *sakka* (writer)   さっき *sakki* (just now)

まっくら *makkura* (total darkness)

せっけん *sekken* (soap)   けっこん *kekkon* (marriage)

Sa-gyo	っさ -ssa	っし -sshi	っす -ssu	っせ -sse	っそ -sso

Examples:

いっさい *issai* (all)   ざっし *zasshi* (magazine)

まっすぐ *massugu* (straight)   たっせい *tassei* (achievement)

はっそう *hasso* (mailing)

Ta-gyo	った -tta	っち -tchi	っつ -ttsu	って -tte	っと -tto

Examples:

りったい *rittai* (solid body)   あっち *atchi* (there)

みっつ *mittsu* (three)   こぎって *kogitte* (check)

しっと *shitto* (jealousy)

Ha-gyo	っは -hha	っひ -hhi	っふ -ffu	っへ -hhe	っほ -hho

Examples:

あっはっは ahhahha   いっひっひ ihhihhi

うっふっふ uffuffu   へっへっへ hehhehhe

ほっほっほ hohhohho

(These are onomatopoeia for laughters.)

Pa-gyo	っぱ -ppa	っぴ -ppi	っぷ -ppu	っぺ -ppe	っぽ -ppo

Examples:

はっぱ *happa* (leaf)   じっぴ *jippi* (actual cost)

きっぷ *kippu* (ticket)   ほっぺた *hoppeta* (cheek)

しっぽ *shippo* (tail)

1. The small-size (tsu) is almost always silent with a time duration the same as one syllable and you stop the breath at that time. The double consonant of *chi* is not *cchi* but *tchi*. In Hepburn Romanization *chi* is included in the above group as one syllable of *ta-gyo*, and *fu* is also included as one of *ha-gyo* exceptionally. The double-consonant words of *ha-gyo* are chiefly loan-words of foreign origin and these words are written in Katakana; バッハ Bahha (J.S. Bach), マッハ Mahha (Mach). It is difficult to find sample words having double consonants of *ha-gyo* of Japanese origin because they usually change to *pa-gyo* by euphonic change and all of the above sample words of *ha-gyo* are laughing voice sounds.

ha は (leaf): *ha* + *ha* = *haha* → *happa* はっぱ (leaves)

hi ひ (cost): *jitsu* じつ (real) + *hi*= *jitsuhi* → *jippi* じっぴ (real cost)

fu ふ (cloth): *shitsu* しつ (wet) + *fu*= *shitsufu* → *shippu* しっぷ
(compress)

hei へい (together with): *gatsu* がっ (unite) + *hei*= *gatsuhei* →
→ *gappei* がっぺい (union)

hō ほう (firearm): *tetsu* てつ (iron) + *hō*= *tetsuhō* → *teppō* てっぽう
(gun)

2. Concerning the double *nn* the first *n* (ん) is one syllable and the second *n* is the first part of the following syllable.

Shi · n · ne · n (new year)   *a · n · na · i* (guide)

しんねん   あんない

za · n · ne · n (regret)   *mi · n · na* (all)

ざんねん   みんな

An *n* occuring before *b, m,* and *p* changes to an *m* sound in speech and is so written when romanized:

shi · n · bu · n → *shimbun* しんぶん (newspaper)

shi · n · pa · i → *shimpai* しんぱい (worry)

e · n · pi · tsu → *empitsu* えんぴつ (pencil)

a · n · ma → *amma* あんま (massage)

a · n · ma · ri → *ammari* あんまり (too much)

ka · n · mu · ri → *kammuri* かんむり (crown)

So the first *m* of *mm* is the changed form from *n* and the second *m* is the first part of the following syllable.

The first *n* of each double consonat is written as ん in Hiragana.

Answers to Exercises on pages 134-135.

page 134

100	ひゃく	200	にひゃく
300	さんびゃく	400	よんひゃく
500	ごひゃく	600	ろっぴゃく
700	ななひゃく	800	はっぴゃく
900	きゅうひゃく	1,000	せん
2,000	にせん	3,000	さんぜん
4,000	よんせん	5,000	ごせん

page 135

6,000	ろくせん	7,000	ななせん
8,000	はっせん	9,000	きゅうせん
10,000	いちまん	20,000	にまん
30,000	さんまん	40,000	よんまん
50,000	ごまん	60,000	ろくまん
70,000	ななまん	80,000	はちまん
90,000	きゅうまん	100,000	じゅうまん
1,000,000	ひゃくまん	100,000,000	いちおく

Exercises

● Trace over the dotted lines.

diary
ni · kki

absolutely
ze · tta · i · ni

postage stamp
yū · bi · n · ki · tte

handle
to · tte

plan
se · kke · i

marriage
ke · kko · n

school
ga · kkō

be surprised at
bi · kku · ri · su · ru

scratch
hi・kka・ku

removal
hi・kko・shi

quickly
te・tto・ri・ba・ya・ku

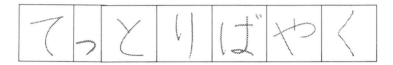

mainly
mo・ppa・ra

masterpiece
ke・ssa・ku

entirely
ma・tta・ku

more
i・ssō

determine
ke・sshi・n・su・ru

clearly
ku・kki・ri

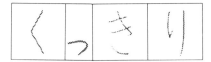

pull
hi・ppa・ru

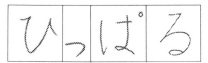

more
mo・tto

pharmacy
ya・kkyo・ku

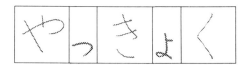

lifetime
i・sshō

husband
o・tto

encyclopedia
hya・kka・ji・te・n

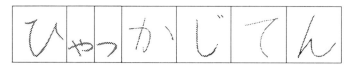

deep red
ma・kka

together
i・ssho・ni

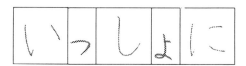

peppermint
ha • kka

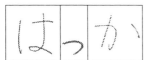

train
re • ssha

eager
ne • sshi • n • na

national flag
ko • kki

boiling water
ne • ttō

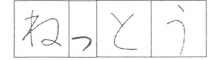

the Diet
ko • kka • i

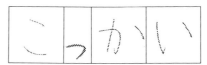

carry out
ji • kkō • su • ru

fail
shi • ppa • i • su • ru

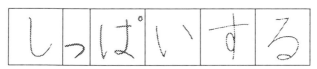

writer
sa・kka

lively
ka・ppa・tsu・na

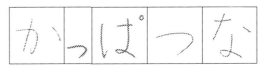

result
ke・kka

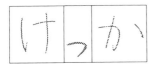

on the contrary
ka・e・tte

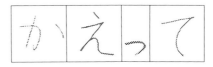

prices
bu・kka

limited express
to・kkyū

fault
ke・tte・n

parenthesis
ka・kko

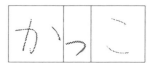

assent to
na・tto・ku・su・ru

a week
i・sshū・ka・n

straight
ma・ssu・gu・na

musical instrument
ga・kki

there
a・tchi

pure white
ma・sshi・ro・na

publish
ha・kkō・su・ru

discover
ha・kke・n・su・ru

Contracted Syllables (Yōon)

ki + ya-gyo	きゃ kya	きゅ kyu	きょ kyo
gi + ya-gyo	ぎゃ gya	ぎゅ gyu	ぎょ gyo
shi + ya-gyo	しゃ sha	しゅ shu	しょ sho
ji + ya-gyo	じゃ ja	じゅ ju	じょ jo
chi + ya-gyo	ちゃ cha	ちゅ chu	ちょ cho
ji + ya-gyo	ぢゃ ja	ぢゅ ju	ぢょ jo
ni + ya-gyo	にゃ nya	にゅ nyu	にょ nyo
hi + ya-gyo	ひゃ hya	ひょ hyu	ひょ hyo
bi + ya-gyo	びゃ bya	びゅ byu	びょ byo
pi + ya-gyo	ぴゃ pya	ぴゅ pyu	ぴょ pyo
mi + ya-gyo	みゃ mya	みゅ myu	みょ myo
ri + ya-gyo	りゃ rya	りゅ ryu	りょ ryo

Yōon is a compound and contracted sound of two basic Hiragana. Each Yōon is formed by a compound of one of eleven syllables of *i-dan* (ki, gi, shi, ji, chi, ni, hi, bi, pi, mi and ri) into three syllables of *ya-gyo* (ya, yu and yo). Regarding the writing of Yōon in Hiragana the *ya-gyo* syllable should be written in a small size. The Romanization of *i* in the first syllable is omitted in compounds of two syllables.

For example:

き ＋ や ＝ きや ⟶ きゃ
ki   *ya*   *kiya – i*   *kya*

In case the first syllable is *chi, ji* or *shi*, in addition to *i* of the first syllable, *y* of the last syllable is also omitted.

ち ＋ や ＝ ちや → ちゃ
chi   *ya*   *chiya – i, y*   *cha*

じ ＋ ゆ ＝ じゆ → じゅ
ji   *yu*   *jiyu – i, y*   *ju*

し ＋ よ ＝ しよ → しょ
shi   *yo*   *shiyo – i, y*   *sho*

Long Vowels in Contracted Syllables (Yōon)

Long vowels in contracted syllables occur in the syllables of *a-dan*, *u-dan* and *o-dan*.

1. Long Vowels in the Syllables of *a-dan*

Basic Yōon (Contracted Syllables)

Basic sounds	① きゃ kya	② しゃ sha	③ ちゃ cha	④ にゃ nya	⑤ ひゃ hya	⑥ みゃ mya	⑦ りゃ rya
Long sounds	⑧ きゃあ kyā kyaa	⑨ しゃあ shā shaa	⑩ ちゃあ chā chaa	⑪ にゃあ nyā nyaa	⑫ ひゃあ hyā hyaa	⑬ みゃあ myā myaa	⑭ りゃあ ryā ryaa

Voiced and Semi-Voiced Yōon

Basic sounds	⑮ ぎゃ gya	⑯ じゃ ja	⑰ ぢゃ ja		⑱ びゃ bya	⑲ ぴゃ pya
Long sounds	⑳ ぎゃあ gyā gyaa	㉑ じゃあ jā jaa	㉒ ぢゃあ jā jaa		㉓ びゃあ byā byaa	㉔ ぴゃあ pyā pyaa

Examples:

① きゃく *kyaku* (guest)　② しゃしん *shashin* (photograph)

③ ちゃ *cha* (tea)　④ にゃんこ *nyanko* (kitty 〔child's word〕)

⑤ ひゃく *hyaku* (one hundred)　⑥ みゃく *myaku* (pulse)

⑦ しょうりゃく *shōryaku* (abridgment)

⑧ きゃあきゃあ *kyā-kyā* (scream)

⑨ しゃあしゃあ *shā-shā* (shameless)

⑩ ちゃあはん *chāhan* (fried rice)

⑪ にゃあにゃあ *nyā-nyā* (mew)

⑫ ひゃあ！ *hyā!* (exclamatory sound)　⑬　*

⑭ ありゃあ！ *aryā!* (exclamatory word)

⑮ ぎゃく *gyaku* (reverse)

⑯&⑰ じゃくてん *jakuten* (weak point)

⑱ さんびゃく *sambyaku* (three hundred)

⑲ はっぴゃく *happyaku* (eight-hundred)

⑳ ぎゃあぎゃあ *gyāgyā* (squawk)

㉑&㉒ 「じゃあ」 *Jā* ("Well")　㉓&㉔　*

* ＝No appropriate word in Japanese with this sound.

2. Long Vowels in the Syllables of *u-dan*

Basic Yōon

Basic sounds	① きゅ kyu	② しゅ shu	③ ちゅ chu	④ にゅ nyu	⑤ ひゅ hyu	⑥ みゅ myu	⑦ りゅ ryu
Long sounds	⑧ きゅう kyū	⑨ しゅう shū	⑩ ちゅう chū	⑪ にゅう nyū	⑫ ひゅう hyū	⑬ みゅう myū	⑭ りゅう ryū

Voiced and Semi-Voiced Yōon

Basic sounds	⑮ ぎゅ gyu	⑯ じゅ ju	⑰ ぢゅ ju		⑱ びゅ byu	⑲ ぴゅ pyu
Long sounds	⑳ ぎゅう gyū	㉑ じゅう jū	㉒ ぢゅう jū		㉓ びゅう byū	㉔ ぴゅう pyū

Examples:

① きゅっと *kyutto* (squeeze or press tightly)

② しゅっぱん *shuppan* (publication)

③ ちゅんちゅん *chun-chun* (birds' twitterings)

④ にゅるにゅる *nyuru-nyuru* (long, thin slippery object sliding continuously)

⑤ ひゅるひゅる *hyuru-hyuru* (go whizzing by)

⑥ No appropriate word in Japanese with this sound.

⑦ りゅっくさっく, リュックサック *ryukkusakku* (rucksack)

⑧ きゅうこう *kyūkō* (express) ⑨ しゅうかん *shūkan* (custom)

⑩ ちゅうしゃ *chūsha* (injection)

⑪ にゅうじょう *nyūjō* (entrance)

⑫ ひゅうひゅう *hyū-hyū* (whistle of the wind)

⑬ みゅうじかる, ミュージカル *myūjikaru* (musical comedy)

⑭ りゅう *ryū* (dragon) ⑮ ぎゅっと *gyūtto* (firmly)

⑯&⑰ じゅんばん *jumban* (turn) ⑱ びゅん *byun* (zip)

⑲ ぴゅっぴゅっと *pyuppyutto* (spouting sound)

⑳ ぎゅうにゅう *gyūnyū* (milk)

㉑&㉒ じゅうどう *Jūdō* (Judo)

㉓ びゅうびゅう *byūbyū* (whistle of the wind)

㉔ ぴゅうぴゅう *pyūpyū* (whistle of the wind)

Answers to exercises on pages 109–110.

page 109

1.	e o kaku	7.	kiku	12.	osu
2.	tsukuru	8.	sumu	13.	hipparu
3.	haneru	9.	ugokasu	14.	mazeru
4.	tobu	10.	asobu	15.	kurikaesu
5.	manabu	11.	yubisasu	16.	suki
6.	kau				

page 110

17.	aisuru	23.	nuu	29.	denwa-suru
18.	noru	24.	furueru	30.	matsu
19.	hiroiageru	25.	akushu-suru	31.	wakeru
20.	niru	26.	haku	32.	sakebu
21.	utau	27.	benkyō-suru	33.	miseru
22.	ryōri-suru	28.	omou		

3. Long Vowels in the Syllables of *o-dan*

Basic Yōon

Basic sounds	きょ ① kyo	しょ ② sho	ちょ ③ cho	にょ ④ nyo	ひょ ⑤ hyo	みょ ⑥ myo	りょ ⑦ ryo
Long sounds	きょう ⑧ kyō kyoo	しょう ⑨ shō shoo	ちょう ⑩ chō choo	にょう ⑪ nyō nyoo	ひょう ⑫ hyō hyoo	みょう ⑬ myō myoo	りょう ⑭ ryō ryoo

Basic sounds	ぎょ ⑮ gyo	じょ ⑯ jo	ぢょ ⑰ jo		びょ ⑱ byo	ぴょ ⑲ pyo
Long sounds	ぎょう ⑳ gyō gyoo	じょう ㉑ jō joo	ぢょう ㉒ jō joo		びょう ㉓ byō byoo	ぴょう ㉔ pyō pyoo

Examples:

① きょか *kyoka* (permission)   ② しょくじ *shokuji* (meal)

② ちょきん *chokin* (savings)

④ にょきにょき *nyokinyoki* (one after another)

⑤ ひょっこり *hyokkori* (unexpectedly)   ⑥ *

⑦ りょかん *ryokan* (hotel)   ⑧ きょう *kyō* (today)

⑨ しょうねん *shōnen* (boy)

⑩ ちょうちん *chōchin* (paper lantern)

⑪ にょうぼう *nyōbō* (wife)　　⑫ とうひょう *tōhyō* (vote)

⑬ みょうばん *myōban* (tomorrow evening)

⑭ りょうきん *ryōkin* (charge, fare)

⑮ ぎょこう *gyokō* (fishing port)

⑯ & ⑰ じょこうする *jokō suru* (go slow)　　⑱ *

⑲ ぴょんぴょん *pyonpyon* (hop)　　⑳ ぎょうじ *gyōji* (event)

㉑ & ㉒ じょうき *jōki* (steam)　　㉓ びょうき *byōki* (sickness)

㉔ はっぴょう *happyō* (announcement)

＊＝No appropriate word in Japanese with this sound.

Answers to exercises on pages 111– 113

page 111

34. hohoemu	40. ryokō-suru	46. nageru
35. sawaru	41. furu	47. hōmon-suru
36. te ni toru	42. arau	48. sora o tobu
37. tsukeru	43. jitto miru	49. tanomu
38. oshieru	44. oyogu	50. kaeru
39. kesu	45. musubu	51. okiru

page 112

52. mezameru	57. warau	62. kau	66. suwaru
53. neru	58. naku	63. uru	67. kizamu
54. aruku	59. hanasu	64. harau	68. kowasu
55. hashiru	60. ageru	65. tatsu	69. yomu
56. tomaru	61. morau		

page 113

70. kaku	75. miru	79. katazukeru	83. shuppatsu-suru
71. kiru	76. sagasu	80. motsu	
72. nugu	77. akeru	81. naosu	84. ayamaru
73. daku	78. tojiru	82. hajimaru	85. iku
74. sewa o suru			

Exercises

● Trace over the dotted lines.

get a job
shū·sho·ku·su·ru

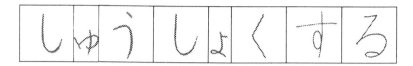

cross
jū·ji·ka

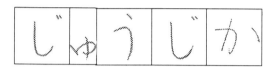

lunch
chū·sho·ku

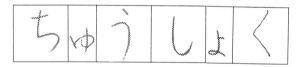

fluent
ryū·chō·na

high class
jō·tō·no

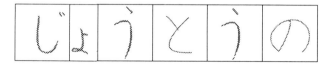

surface
hyō · me · n

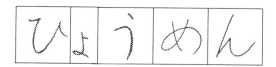

library
to · sho · ka · n

both
ryō · hō

negotiate
kō · shō · su · ru

understand
ryō · ka · i · su · ru

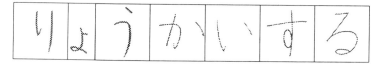

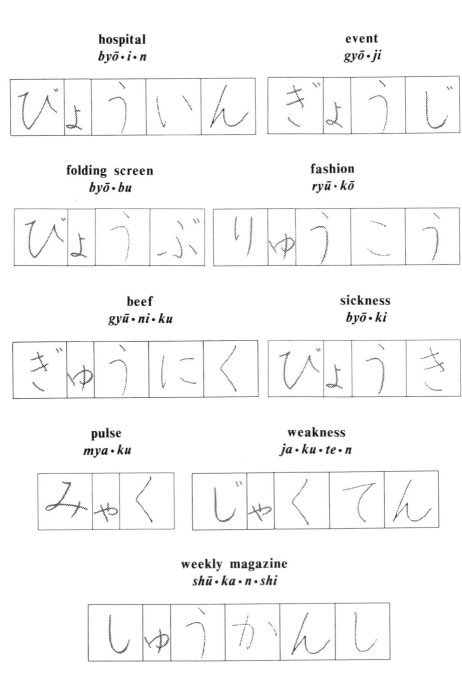

hospital
byō・i・n

びょういん

event
gyō・ji

ぎょうじ

folding screen
byō・bu

びょうぶ

fashion
ryū・kō

りゅうこう

beef
gyū・ni・ku

ぎゅうにく

sickness
byō・ki

びょうき

pulse
mya・ku

みゃく

weakness
ja・ku・te・n

じゃくてん

weekly magazine
shū・ka・n・shi

しゅうかんし

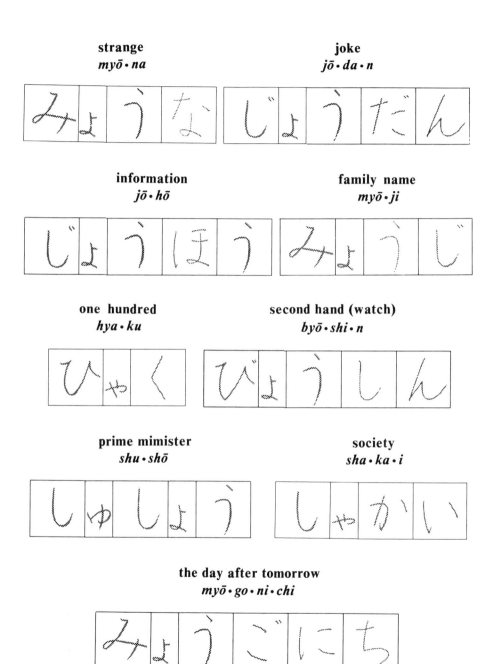

strange
myō・na

joke
jō・da・n

information
jō・hō

family name
myō・ji

one hundred
hya・ku

second hand (watch)
byō・shi・n

prime mimister
shu・shō

society
sha・ka・i

the day after tomorrow
myō・go・ni・chi

public holiday
shu · ku · ji · tsu

meal
sho · ku · ji

vacation
kyū · ka

sick person
byō · ni · n

restaurant
sho · ku · dō

baseball
ya · kyū

occupation
sho · ku · gyō

express train
kyū · kō · re · ssha

inject
chū・sha・su・ru

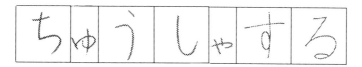

birthday
ta・n・jō・bi

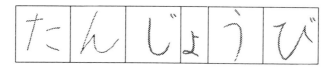

school lesson
ju・gyō

enough
jū・bu・n・na

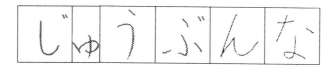

important
jū・da・i・na

parents
ryō · shi · n

cooking
ryō · ri

territory
ryō · do

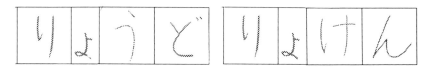

passport
ryo · ke · n

pay
kyū · ryō

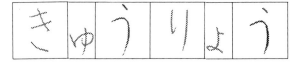

emergency
ki · n · kyū

atomic energy
gen · shi · ryo · ku

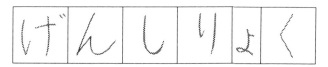

education
kyō・i・ku

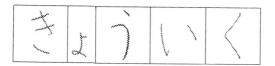

guest
kya・ku

railroad train
ki・sha

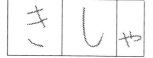

center
chū・ō

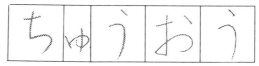

lantern
chō・chi・n

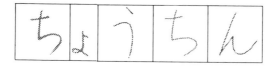

girl
shō・jo

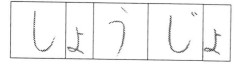

company
ka・i・sha

thank
ka・n・sha・su・ru

president
sha · chō

tea
kō · cha

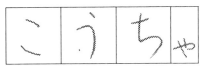

departure
shu · ppa · tsu

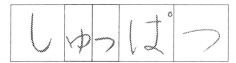

photography
sha · shi · n

old type
kyū · shi · ki

introduce
shō · ka · i · su · ru

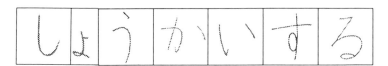

employee
jū · gyō · i · n

middle age
chū・ne・n

ちゅうねん

ten
jū

じゅう

electric car
den・sha

でんしゃ

last year
kyo・ne・n

きょねん

practice
re・n・shū

れんしゅう

urgent
shi・kyū

しきゅう

boy
shō・ne・n

しょうねん

milk
gyū・nyū

ぎゅうにゅう

advice
chū·ko·ku

parrot
ō·mu

Japanese inn
ryo·kan

reputation
hyō·ba·n

announcement
ha·ppyō

cucumber
kyū·ri

excellent
jō·de·ki

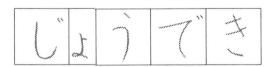

honest
shō·ji·ki·na

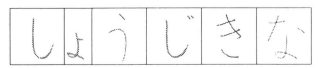

HOW TO WRITE SENTENCES IN HIRAGANA

Now that you have learned how to write words in Hiragana, the subsequent lessons are on learning how to write sentences. Before that you had better know some rules about the writing of sentences:

1. Notes on Some Particles

The particle *wa* following a noun or pronoun shows the nominative case. It is pronounced [wa] but is written as は (ha) in Hiragana, not わ (wa). The particle *e* shows direction and is attached to a noun or pronoun. It is pronounced [e] but is represented by へ (he) rather than え (e). The particle *o* is pronounced [o] and attached to a noun or pronoun it shows the direct object. It is written with を not お.

Kon'nichi wa. (Hello)
こんにちは。

Sore wa nan desu ka? (What is it?)
それはなんですか。

Kore wa watakushi no hon desu. (This is my book.)
これ は わたくし の ほん です。

Watakushi wa gakusei desu. (I am a student.)
わたくし は がくせい です。

Kanojo wa watakushi no ane desu. (She is my elder sister.)
かのじょ は わたくし の あねです。

Doko e ikimasu ka? (Where are you going?)
どこへ いきます か。

Gakkō e ikimasu. (I am going to school.)
がっこう へ いきます。

Keisatsu e ikimasu. (I am going to the police station.)
けいさつ へ いきます。

Are o misete kudasai. (Please show me that.)
あれ を みせて ください。

Anata wa ano hito o shitte imasu ka? (Do you know him?)
あなた は あの ひと を しって いますか。

Kore o kudasai. (Please give me this.)
これ を ください。

2. Punctuation

。 *Kuten:* this mark is equivalent to the period in English but is not a black circle and it is called *maru* (circle) informally.

、 *Tōten:* this mark equals to the English comma and is usually called *ten* (dot) informally. Recently, the English comma is used as a *toten* when writing horizontally.

「 」 ⌐ *Kagi-kakko:* these brackets are Japanese quotation marks and they are written as 「 」 for writing horizontally and ⌐ for writing vertically.

Please note the position of each mark for both writing horizontally and vertically in the examples on page 107.

The use of exclamation mark and question mark is not permitted in formal writing but they are used widely in almost all of novels or informal writing like as letters.

3. Plural Forms in Japanese

In Japanese there are no plural form of nouns. Some words become plural form by adding a suffix (-tachi, -gata or -ra). These suffixes are attached chiefly to human or other living beings.

kare (he) + *-ra* = *karera* (they)

かれ　　ら　かれら

kore (this) + *-ra* = *korera* (these)

これ　　ら　これら

anata (you) + *-tachi* [*-gata*] = *anatatachi* [*anatagata*]

あなた　たち［がた］あなたたち (pl. you)

［あなたがた］

gakusei (student) + *-tachi* = *gakuseitachi* (students)

がくせい　　たち　がくせいたち

kodomo (child) + *-tachi* = *kodomotachi* (children)

こども　　　たち　こどもたち

sensei (teacher) + *-gata* = *senseigata* (teachers)

せんせい　　がた　せんせいがた

Note: the suffix -gata is the polite form of expression.

4. Writing Horizontally and Vertically (Yokogaki and Tategaki)

There are two ways of writing Japanese: Yokogaki (writing horizontally) and Tategaki (writing vertically). Until now, you have studied Yokogaki, which is used in writing English.

In this section, models will appear for both styles. Note that Tategaki is written from top to bottom and subsequent lines continue from right to left.

●Some Model Examples of Punctuation, Sokuon and Yōon

Yokogaki よこがき
(Writing Horizontally)

Sokuon (Double Consonants)

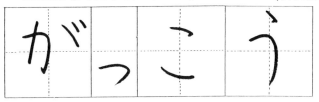

Kagikakko (Brackets) and Kuten (Period)

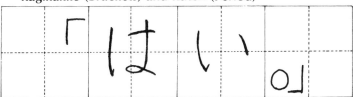

Yōon (Contracted Sound)

Tategaki たてがき
(Writing Vertically)

そくおん

かぎかっこ＋くてん

ようおん

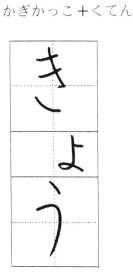

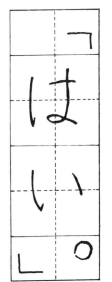

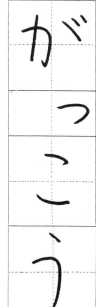

Yokogaki (Writing Horizontally)

Tategaki (Writing Vertically)

Tōten (Comma)
とうてん

Kuten (Period) くてん ▶

Yōon (Contracted Sound)

ようおん

Writing Instruction for Voiced and Semi-Voiced Syllables ▶

Exercises with Basic Verbs

● Trace over the dotted examples, read them and then write them in Roman letters.

Answers are on pages 89 and 91.

1. えをかく (paint)

_____

2. つくる (make)

_____

3. はねる (hop)

_____

4. とぶ (jump)

_____

5. まなぶ (learn)

_____

6. かう (keep a pet)

_____

7. きく (listen)

_____

8. すむ (live)

_____

9. うごかす (move)

_____

10. あそぶ (play)

_____

11. ゆびさす (point)

_____

12. おす (push)

_____

13. ひっぱる (pull)

_____

14. まぜる (mix)

_____

15. くりかえす (repeat)

16. すき (like)

_____

_____

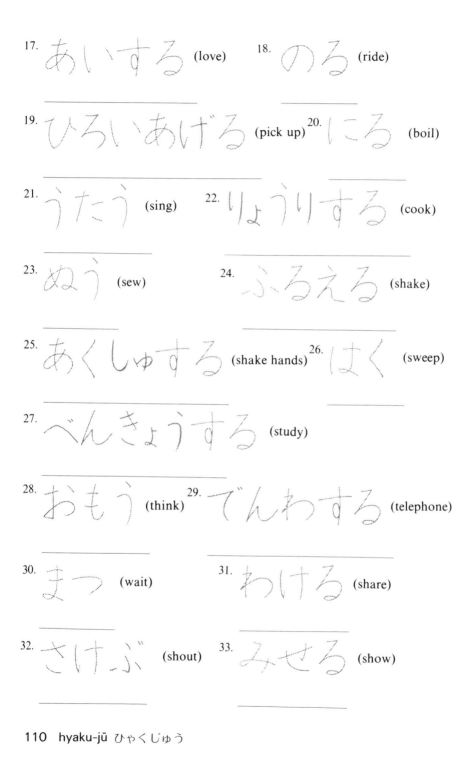

17. あいする (love) 18. のる (ride)

19. ひろいあげる (pick up) 20. にる (boil)

21. うたう (sing) 22. りょうりする (cook)

23. ぬう (sew) 24. ふるえる (shake)

25. あくしゅする (shake hands) 26. はく (sweep)

27. べんきょうする (study)

28. おもう (think) 29. でんわする (telephone)

30. まつ (wait) 31. わける (share)

32. さけぶ (shout) 33. みせる (show)

34. ほほえむ (smile)

35. さわる (touch)

36. てにとる (take)

37. つける (turn on)

38. おしえる (teach)

39. けす (turn off)

40. りょこうする (travel)

41. ふる (wave)

42. あらう (wash)

43. じっとみる (stare at)

44. およぐ (swim)

45. むすぶ (tie)

46. なげる (throw)

47. ほうもんする (visit)

48. そらをとぶ (fly)

49. たのむ (ask)

50. かえる (return)

51. おきる (get up)

52. めざめる (wake up)　53. ねる (sleep)

54. あるく (walk)　55. はしる (run)

56. とまる (stop)　57. わらう (laugh)

58. なく (cry)　59. はなす (talk)

60. あげる (give)　61. もらう (get)

62. かう (buy)　63. うる (sell)

64. はらう (pay)　65. たつ (stand up)

66. すわる (sit down)　67. きざむ (cut)

68. こわす (break)　69. よむ (read)

70. かく (write)

71. きる (put on)

72. ぬぐ (take off)

73. だく (embrace, hug)

74. せわをする (look after)

75. みる (look at)

76. さがす (look for)

77. あける (open)

78. とじる (shut)

79. かたづける (put away)

80. もつ (have)

81. なおす (repair)

82. はじまる (begin)

83. しゅっぱつする (leave)

84. あやまる (apologize)

85. いく (go)

● Complete the words/sentences by tracing over the dotted Hiragana syllables and filling in the blank squares.

Exercises with

come

kuru

く｜る

kimasu

き｜ま｜す

I'll come again next week. *Watakushi wa mata raishū kimasu.*
わたくしはまたらいしゅうきます。

They 'll come along later. *Karera wa ato kara kuru deshō.*
かれらはあとからくるでしょう。

Mr. Tanaka will not come so soon.
Tanaka-san wa sugu niwa konai deshō.
たなかさんはすぐにはこないでしょう。

Mr. Watanabe is coming here the day after tomorrow.
Watanabe-san wa assatte koko ni kimasu.

わたなべさんはあさってここにきます。

Please come to the station at seven o'clock.
Sono eki ni shichi-ji ni kite kudasai.

そのえきにしちじにきてください。

Do you come to school by bicycle?
Gakkō niwa jitensha de kuruno desu ka?

がっこうにはじてんしゃでくるのですか。

The bus comes every 10 minutes.
Basu wa juppun goto ni kimasu.

ばす*はじゅっぷんごとにきます。　　　＊バス

ば			ゆ	ぷ			と

	き			

When did you come here?
Itsu koko ni kitano desu ka?

いつここにきたのですか。

い			に				で

Mr. Suzuki hasn't come yet.
Suzuki-san wa mada kite imasen.

すずきさんはまだきていません。

	ず				ま	

		せ		

Spring has come.
Haru ga kita.

はるがきた。

The children came running.
Kodomo-tachi wa hashitte yatte kimashita.

こどもたちははしってやってきました。

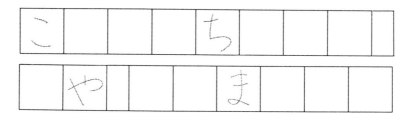

She doesn't come here today.
Kanojo wa kyō wa koko ni kimasen.

かのじょはきょうはここにきません。

● Complete the words/sentences by tracing over the dotted Hiragana
syllables and filling in the blank squares.

(...o) eru (gain)

Exercises with

える

get

kau (buy)

かう

te ni ireru (obtain)

てにいれる

morau (receive)

もらう

I got a letter from his father.
Watakushi wa kare no otōsan kara tegami o moraimashita.

わたくしはかれのおとうさんからてがみをもらい
ました。

I've got a bad cold.
Warui kaze o hiite imasu.

わるいかぜをひいています。

Where will you get the dictionary?
Anata wa doko de jisho o kau no desuka?
あなたはどこでじしょをかうのですか。

| あ | | | ど | | | | し | |

| | | の | | | | | |

I got my watch repaired.
Watakushi wa tokei o naoshite moraimashita.
わたくしは とけいをなおしてもらいました。

| わ | | | は | | | | を |

| | | て | | | ま | |

| | |

I got my hair cut.
Watakushi wa kami o katte moraimashita.
わたしはかみをかってもらいました。

| | た | | | | み | | |

| | も | | ま | | | | |

What time does the train get in?
Ressha wa nanji ni tōchaku shimasuka?

れっしゃはなんじにとうちゃくしますか。

れ				な				と

				し				

How are you getting along?
Dō shite oraremasuka?

どうしておられますか。

ど			お			す

I will get my work finished by seven.
Watashi wa shichiji made ni shigoto o owarasemasu.

わたしはしちじまでにしごとをおわらせます。

わ				ち			

に			を			せ

What time do you get up?
Anata wa nanji ni okimasuka?

あなたはなんじにおきますか。

あ				な				お

			か					

I get up at four every morning.
Watakushi wa maiasa yoji ni okimasu.

わたしはまいあさよじにおきます。

わ				ま				よ

			き					

We got to the theater at nine thirty.
Watakushitachi wa gekijō ni kuji-han ni tsuki mashita.

わたくしたちはげきじょうにくじはんにつきました。

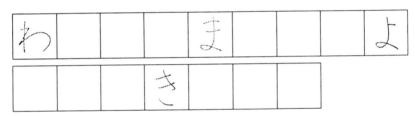

わ				た				き

			く				に	

			し					

We got tired.
Watakushitachi wa tsukaremashita.

わたくしたちはつかれました。

わ				た			か

		た	

You must get ready to start.
Anata wa shuppatsu no jumbi o shinakutewa ikemasen.

あなたはしゅっぱつのじゅんびをしなくてはいけ
ません。

あ			し			の

	び				て

		ま			

Will you get me my umbrella?
Watashi no kasa o mottekite kuremasenka?

わたしのかさをもってきてくれませんか。

わ			か			て

		れ			か	

The policeman got the thief.
Keikan wa sono dorobō o tsukamaemashita.

けいかんはそのどろぼうをつかまえました。

け			は			ろ
		つ			ま	

May I get in your car?
Anata no kuruma ni nottemo ii desu ka?

あなたのくるまにのってもいいですか。

あ			く			の	
	い			か			

Let's get off the bus at the next stop.
Tsugi no teiryūjo de basu o orimashō.   *バス

つぎのていりゅうじょで、ばす*をおりましょう。

つ			い			じ		
	、	ば			り			
う	

● Complete the words/sentences by tracing over the dotted Hiragana syllables and filling in the blank squares.

Exercises with **take**

te ni toru
(hold with the hands)

てにとる

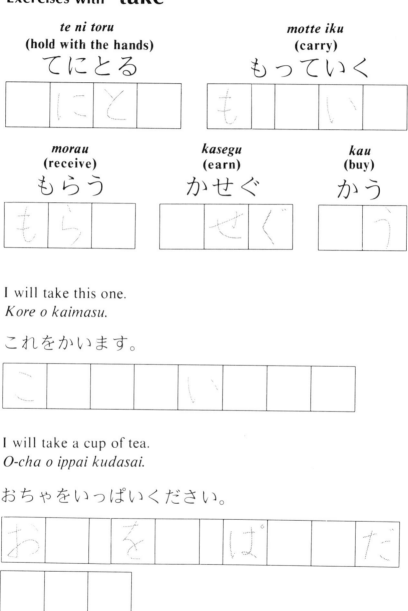

motte iku
(carry)

もっていく

morau
(receive)

もらう

kasegu
(earn)

かせぐ

kau
(buy)

かう

I will take this one.
Kore o kaimasu.

これをかいます。

I will take a cup of tea.
O-cha o ippai kudasai.

おちゃをいっぱいください。

Mr. Ito is taking a bath now.
Itō-san wa ima o-furo ni haitte imasu.

いとうさんはいまおふろにはいっています。

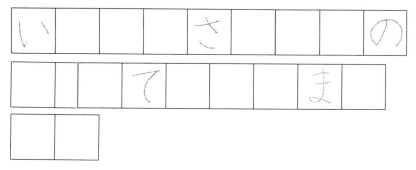

Mr. Inoue took her by the hand.
Inoue-san wa kanojo no te o torimashita.

いのうえさんはかのじょのてをとりました。

Please take your seat.
Dōzo seki ni tsuite kudasai.

どうぞせきについてください。

It takes six minutes to walk from here to the city hall.
Koko kara shiyakusho made aruite roppun kakarimasu.

ここからしやくしょまであるいてろっぷんかか
ります。

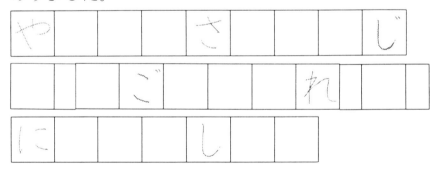

Mr. Yamamoto took the 4:15 train.
Yamamoto-san wa yo-ji jū-go-fun no ressha ni norimashita.

やまもとさんはよじじゅうごふんのれっしゃに
のりました。

May I take a copy of this catalog?
Kono katarogu o ichi-bu moratte ii desuka?

＊カタログ

このかたろぐ を いちぶもらっていいですか。

Mr. Kobayashi takes 400,000 yen a month.

Kobayashi-san wa tsuki ni yon-jū-man yen kasegimasu.

こばやしさんはつきによんじゅうまんえんかせ
ぎます。

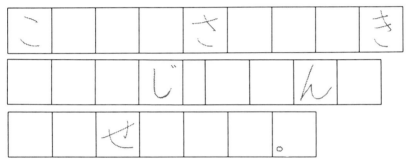

How long does it take you to get to your office?

Kaisha made dore kurai jikan ga kakari masuka?

かいしゃまでどれくらいじかんがかかりますか。

It takes me about 45 minutes by subway.
Chikatetsu de yaku yon-jū-go-fun kakari masu.

ちかてつでやくよんじゅうごふんかかります。

ち			で				ん

		ご				か	

	。

I had my picture taken.
Shashin o totte moraimashita.

しゃしんをとってもらいました。

し			を			も	

		し			

It took me two years to write this book.
Kono hon o kaku noni ni-nen kakarimashita.

このほんをかくのににねんかかりました。

こ			を				に

		か				し	

This bus will take you to the library.
Kono basu ni noreba toshokan ni ikemasu.

このばす*にのればとしょかんにいけます。　　*バス

Ms. Kimura takes care of her grandmother.
Kimura-san wa kanojo no obāsan no mendō o miteimasu.

きむらさんはかのじょのおばあさんのめんどうを
みています。

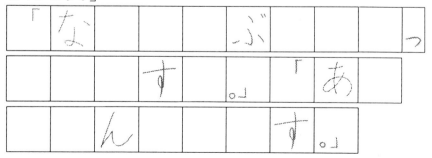

"What paper do you take?" "I take the Asahi."
"Nani shimbun o totte imasuka?" "Asahi Shimbun desu."

「なにしんぶんをとっていますか。」「あさひしん
ぶんです。」

Writing Vertically (Tategaki)

● Chinese-Derived Numerals

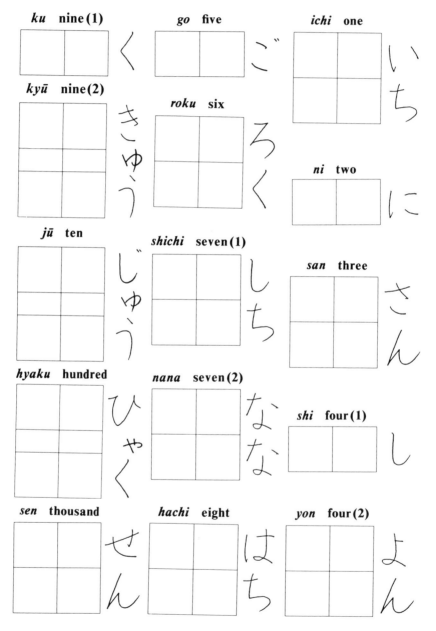

ku nine (1)

く

go five

ご

ichi one

いち

kyū nine (2)

きゅう

roku six

ろく

ni two

に

jū ten

じゅう

shichi seven (1)

しち

san three

さん

hyaku hundred

ひゃく

nana seven (2)

なな

shi four (1)

し

sen thousand

せん

hachi eight

はち

yon four (2)

よん

● Read the Romanized Japanese and write the Hiragana words twice in the squares provided.

● Native Japanese Numerals

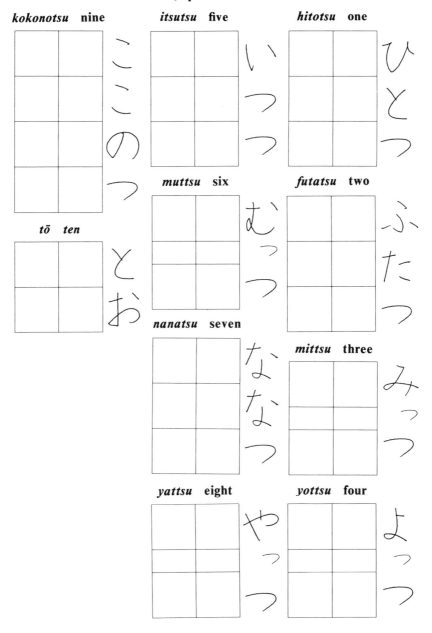

kokonotsu nine

こ
こ
の
つ

itsutsu five

い
つ
つ

hitotsu one

ひ
と
つ

tō ten

と
お

muttsu six

む
っ
つ

futatsu two

ふ
た
つ

nanatsu seven

な
な
つ

mittsu three

み
っ
つ

yattsu eight

や
っ
つ

yottsu four

よ
っ
つ

Exercises

1. Kyō wa kumotte imasu.   It is cloudy today.

2. Kinō wa ame deshita.   It was raining yesterday.

3. Asu wa hareru deshō.   It will be fine tomorrow.

● Read the Romanized Japanese and write the Hiragana words twice in the squares provided.

1. "Mado o akete kudasai."   "Please open the window."

2. "Kōen ni ikimashō."   "Let's go to the park."

3. "Ima nanji desuka?"   "What time is it now?"

1.
「まどをあけてください。」

2.
「こうえんにいきましょう。」

3.
「いま、なんじですか。」

● Read the Romanized Japanese and fill in the squares using Hiragana words.

● Cardinal Numbers

Answers are on page 77.

100
hyaku

200
ni-hyaku

300
sambyaku

400
yon-hyaku

500
go-hyaku

600
roppyaku

700
nana-hyaku

800
happyaku

900
kyū-hyaku

1,000
sen

2,000
ni-sen

3,000
san-zen

4,000
yon-sen

5,000
go-sen

6,000
roku-sen

7,000
nana-sen

8,000
hassen

9,000
kyū-sen

10,000
ichi-man

20,000
ni-man

30,000
san-man

40,000
yon-man

50,000
go-man

60,000
roku-man

70,000
nana-man

80,000
hachi-man

90,000
kyū-man

100,000
jū-man

1,000,000
hyaku-man

100,000,000
ichi-oku

- Read the Romanized Japanese and write the Hiragana words in the squares provided.

- **National Holidays in Japan** *Nihon no saijitsu*

にほんのさいじつ

January 1
ichi-gatsu tsuitachi

いちがつついたち

[ichi jitsu]

いちじつ

New Year's Day *Gantan*

がんたん

January 15
ichi-gatsu jū-go nichi

いちがつじゅうごにち

Coming-of-Age Day
Seijin no hi

せいじんのひ

February 11
ni-gatsu jū-ichi nichi

に｜が｜つ｜じ｜ゅ｜う｜い｜ち｜に｜ち

National Foundation Day
Kenkoku kinenbi

け｜ん｜こ｜く｜き｜ね｜ん｜び

March 20 or 21
san-gatsu hatsuka　　　　　　　　　　*matawa*

さ｜ん｜が｜つ｜は｜つ｜か　ま｜た｜は

ni-ju-ichi nichi

に｜じ｜ゅ｜う｜い｜ち｜に｜ち

Spring Equinox Day
Shumbun no hi

し｜ゅ｜ん｜ぶ｜ん｜の｜ひ

April 29
shi-gatsu ni-jū-ku nichi

し | が | つ | に | じゅ | う | く | に | ち

Emperor's Birthday
Ten'nō tanjōbi

て | ん | の | う | た | ん | じょ | う | び

May 3
go-gatsu mikka

ご | が | つ | み | っ | か

Constitution Day
Kempō kinenbi

け | ん | ぽ | う | き | ね | ん | び

May 5
go gatsu itsuka

ご | が | つ | い | つ | か

Children's Day
Kodomo no hi

こ | ど | も | の | ひ

September 15
ku-gatsu jū-go nichi

く | が | つ | じ | ゅ | う | ご | に | ち

Respect-for-the Aged Day
Keirō no hi

け | い | ろ | う | の | ひ

September 23 or 24
ku-gatsu ni-jū san nichi

く | が | つ | に | じ | ゅ | う | さ | ん | に | ち

matawa

ま | た | は

ni-jū yokka

に | じ | ゅ | う | よ | っ | か

Autumnal Equinox Day
Shūbun no hi

し ゅ う ぶ ん の ひ

October 10
jū-gatsu tōka

じ ゅ う が つ と お か

Sports Day
Taiiku no hi

た い い く の ひ

November 3
jū-ichi-gatsu mikka

じ ゅ う い ち が つ み っ か

Culture Day
Bunka no hi

ぶ ん か の ひ

November 23
jū-ichi-gatsu ni-jū san nichi

じゅういちがつにじゅ

うさんにち

Labor Thanksgiving Day
Kinrō kansha no hi

きんろうかんしゃのひ

My birthday is June 6.
Watakushi no tanjōbi wa roku-gatsu muika desu.

わたくしのたんじょう

びはろくがつむいか

です。

July 4 is Independence Day in America.
Shichi-gatsu yokka wa Amerika no Dokuritsu kinenbi desu.

しちがつよっかはあ

めりか＊のどくりつき

ねんびです。 ＊アメリカ

August is the hottest month in Japan.
Hachi-gatsu wa Nihon dewa ichiban atsui tsuki desu.

はちがつはにほんで

ばいちばんあついつ

き | で | す | 。

We call the 31st of December "Ōmisoka".
Jū-ni-gatsu sanjū-ichi nichi wa "Ōmisoka" to iimasu.

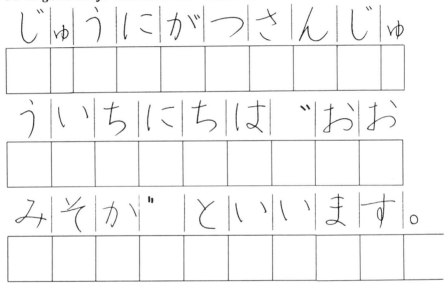

じ | ゅ | う | に | が | つ | さ | ん | じ | ゅ

う | い | ち | に | ち | は | ゛ | お | お

み | そ | か | ゛ | と | い | い | ま | す | 。

Answers to questions on page 144.

● **Answers**   hinichi

1st	tsuitachi or ichi-jitsu	**11th**	jū-ichi-nichi
2nd	futsuka	**12th**	jū-ni-nichi
3rd	mikka	**13th**	jū-san-nichi
4th	yokka	**14th**	jū-yokka
5th	itsuka	**15th**	jū-go-nichi
6th	muika	**16th**	jū-roku-nichi
7th	nanoka	**17th**	jū-shichi-nichi
8th	Yōka	**18th**	jū-hachi-nichi
9th	kokonoka	**19th**	jū-ku-nichi
10th	tōka	**20th**	hatsuka

● Read the following Hiragana words and write them in Romanized Japanese on the line provided.

● **Days of the Month**

ひ に ち

_____

Answers are on page 143.

1st ついたち　いちじつ

_____　_____

2nd ふつか　**3rd** みっか　**4th** よっか

_____　_____　_____

5th いつか　**6th** むいか

_____　_____

7th なのか　**8th** ようか

_____　_____

9th ここのか　**10th** とおか

_____　_____

11th じゅういちにち　_____

12th	じゅうににち
13th	じゅうさんにち
14th	じゅうよっか
15th	じゅうごにち
16th	じゅうろくにち
17th	じゅうしちにち
18th	じゅうはちにち
19th	じゅうくにち
20th	はつか

● Read the Romanized Japanese and write the Hiragana words in the squares provided.

● **Familiar Body Parts**

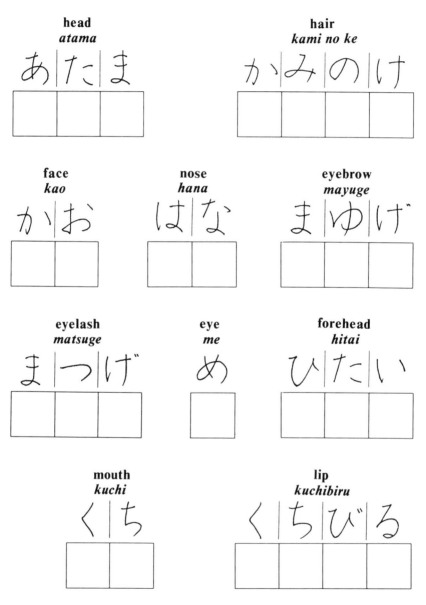

head
atama

あ|た|ま

hair
kami no ke

か|み|の|け

face
kao

か|お

nose
hana

は|な

eyebrow
mayuge

ま|ゆ|げ

eyelash
matsuge

ま|つ|げ

eye
me

め

forehead
hitai

ひ|た|い

mouth
kuchi

く|ち

lip
kuchibiru

く|ち|び|る

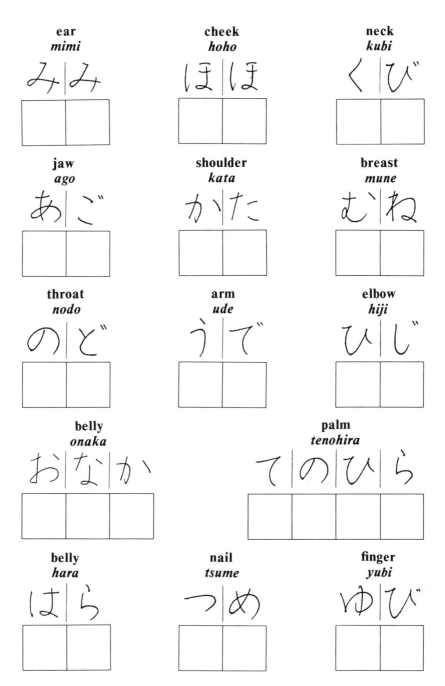

ear
mimi

みみ

cheek
hoho

ほほ

neck
kubi

くび

jaw
ago

あご

shoulder
kata

かた

breast
mune

むね

throat
nodo

のど

arm
ude

うで

elbow
hiji

ひじ

belly
onaka

おなか

palm
tenohira

てのひら

belly
hara

はら

nail
tsume

つめ

finger
yubi

ゆび

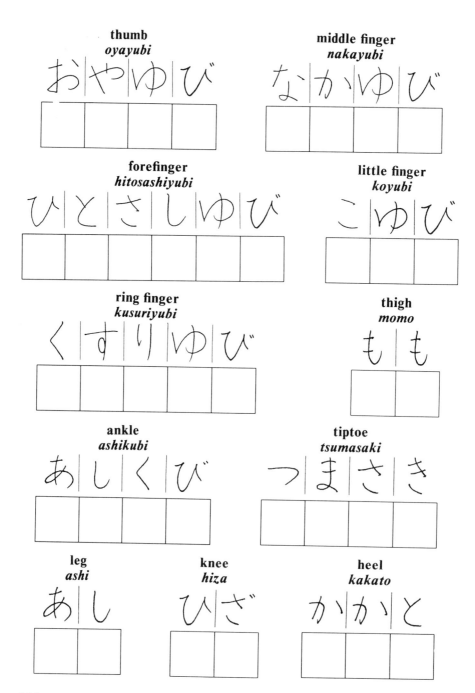

thumb
oyayubi
おやゆび

middle finger
nakayubi
なかゆび

forefinger
hitosashiyubi
ひとさしゆび

little finger
koyubi
こゆび

ring finger
kusuriyubi
くすりゆび

thigh
momo
もも

ankle
ashikubi
あしくび

tiptoe
tsumasaki
つまさき

leg
ashi
あし

knee
hiza
ひざ

heel
kakato
かかと

- Read the Romanized Japanese and write the Hiragana words in the squres provided.

● Main Cities in Japan

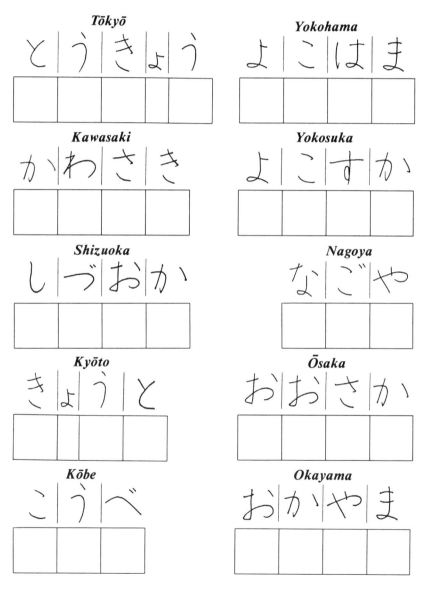

Tōkyō
と | う | き | ょ | う

Yokohama
よ | こ | は | ま

Kawasaki
か | わ | さ | き

Yokosuka
よ | こ | す | か

Shizuoka
し | づ | お | か

Nagoya
な | ご | や

Kyōto
き | ょ | う | と

Ōsaka
お | お | さ | か

Kōbe
こ | う | べ

Okayama
お | か | や | ま

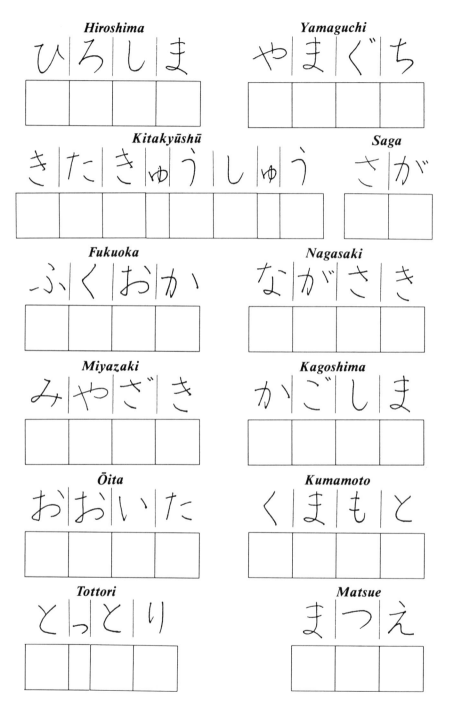

Hiroshima

ひ｜ろ｜し｜ま

Yamaguchi

や｜ま｜ぐ｜ち

Kitakyūshū

き｜た｜き｜ゅう｜し｜ゅう

Saga

さ｜が

Fukuoka

ふ｜く｜お｜か

Nagasaki

な｜が｜さ｜き

Miyazaki

み｜や｜ざ｜き

Kagoshima

か｜ご｜し｜ま

Ōita

お｜お｜い｜た

Kumamoto

く｜ま｜も｜と

Tottori

と｜っ｜と｜り

Matsue

ま｜づ｜え

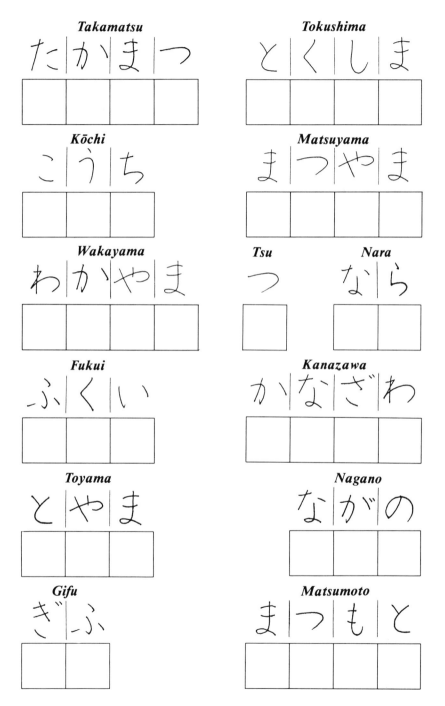

Takamatsu
たかまつ

Tokushima
とくしま

Kōchi
こうち

Matsuyama
まつやま

Wakayama
わかやま

Tsu
つ

Nara
なら

Fukui
ふくい

Kanazawa
かなざわ

Toyama
とやま

Nagano
ながの

Gifu
ぎふ

Matsumoto
まつもと

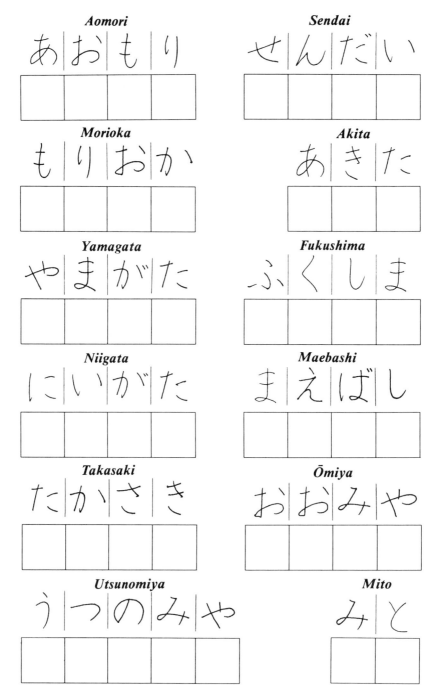

Aomori

あ　お　も　り

Sendai

せ　ん　だ　い

Morioka

も　り　お　か

Akita

あ　き　た

Yamagata

や　ま　が　た

Fukushima

ふ　く　し　ま

Niigata

に　い　が　た

Maebashi

ま　え　ば　し

Takasaki

た　か　さ　き

Ōmiya

お　お　み　や

Utsunomiya

う　つ　の　み　や

Mito

み　と

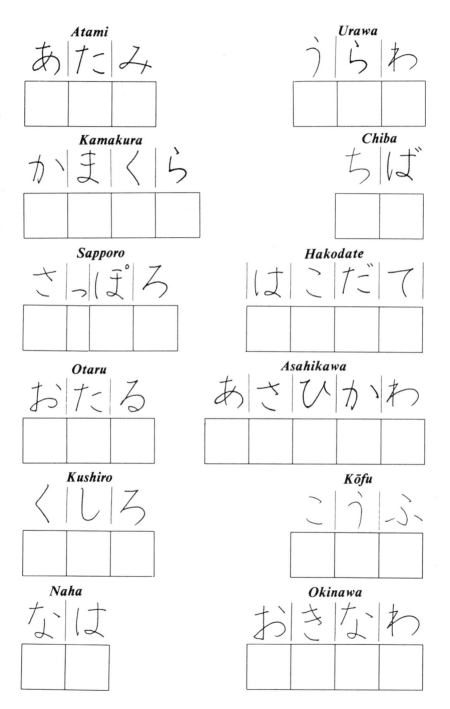

Atami

あ|た|み

Urawa

う|ら|わ

Kamakura

か|ま|く|ら

Chiba

ち|ば

Sapporo

さ|っ|ぽ|ろ

Hakodate

は|こ|だ|て

Otaru

お|た|る

Asahikawa

あ|さ|ひ|か|わ

Kushiro

く|し|ろ

Kōfu

こ|う|ふ

Naha

な|は

Okinawa

お|き|な|わ

Exercise Sheet

Date: Name:

● Please copy these 3 pages to use as exercise sheets.

Date: Name: **Exercise Sheet**

Exercise Sheet   Date: Name: